How much do you know about *Roald Dahl*? Follow along from A to Z!

A is for... Adenoids~ Roald Dahl's adenoids were sliced out by a doctor when he was eight. A perfectly painless procedure, you might think. Wrong! He was wide awake. In 1924, it was quite common for doctors to perform this operation without anesthetic. Arrrrrrgghhh!

B is for... Blabbermouth~ Roald Dahl loved secrets but was terrible at keeping them—he was much too fond of talking.

C is for... Chocolate~ If you were invited to dinner at Roald Dahl's house, at the end of the meal, you'd be offered a red plastic box containing all of Roald Dahl's favorite chocolates: Twix, Kit Kats, Rolos, Smarties, Flakes, and Maltesers. When he was an adult, Roald also used to buy fancy chocolates from a shop in London.

And D is for... DAHL!

Find out more about Roald Dahl
by visiting the Web site at
www.roalddahl.com

PUFFIN BOOKS
Published by the Penguin Group
Penguin Young Readers Group,
345 Hudson Street, New York, New York 10014, U.S.A.
Penguin Group (Canada), 90 Eglinton Avenue East, Suite 700, Toronto, Ontario, Canada M4P 2Y3
(a division of Pearson Penguin Canada Inc.)
Penguin Books Ltd, 80 Strand, London WC2R 0RL, England
Penguin Ireland, 25 St Stephen's Green, Dublin 2, Ireland (a division of Penguin Books Ltd)
Penguin Group (Australia), 250 Camberwell Road, Camberwell, Victoria 3124, Australia
(a division of Pearson Australia Group Pty Ltd)
Penguin Books India Pvt Ltd, 11 Community Centre, Panchsheel Park, New Delhi - 110 017, India
Penguin Group (NZ), 67 Apollo Drive, Rosedale, North Shore 0745, Auckland, New Zealand
(a division of Pearson New Zealand Ltd.)
Penguin Books (South Africa) (Pty) Ltd, 24 Sturdee Avenue, Rosebank, Johannesburg 2196, South Africa

Registered Offices: Penguin Books Ltd, 80 Strand, London WC2R 0RL, England

First published in Great Britain by Penguin Books Ltd., 2004
First published in the United States of America by Viking, a division of Penguin Young Readers Group, 2005
This edition published by Puffin Books, a division of Penguin Young Readers Group, 2007

1 3 5 7 9 10 8 6 4 2

Text copyright © Roald Dahl Nominee, Ltd, 2004
Illustrations copyright © Quentin Blake, 2004
Recipe for Hot-House Eggs on p. 69 previously published in *Roald Dahl's Even More Revolting Recipes* by
Random House Children's Books, 2001
Photographs on p. 96 copyright © Jan Baldwin/Narratives
Photograph on p. 137 copyright © Dorling Kindersley
Photograph on p. 145 copyright © Hulton Archive
All rights reserved
CIP DATA IS AVAILABLE.

Puffin Books ISBN 978-0-14-240934-3

Printed in the United States of America

D is for DAHL

A gloriumptious A-Z guide to the world of ROALD DAHL

PUFFIN BOOKS

ILLUSTRATIONS BY
QUENTIN BLAKE

COMPILED BY WENDY COOLING

The Family Tree

Harald Dahl — Sophie Magdalene Hesselberg
Mormor

Marie   Alf   Roald   Else Asta

Astri

Atty

Louis Ellen

Olivia Tessa   Theo Ophelia   Lucy

Sophie   Phoebe
Clover   Chloë
Luke
Ned

Patricia
Neal

Liccy

Neisha   Charlotte   Lorina

A is for . . .

Aardvark ~ Every A–Z must begin with an aardvark (an African burrowing mammal with long flappy ears and a long nose). Although Roald Dahl didn't feature an aardvark in any of his books, he did invent some crazy creatures—look out for Whangdoodles, Snozzwhangers, and the Pink-Spotted Scrunch.

Adenoids ~ Roald Dahl's adenoids were sliced out by a doctor when he was eight. A perfectly painless procedure, you might think. Wrong! He was wide awake. In 1924, it was quite common for doctors to perform this operation without anesthetic. Arrrrrrgghhh!

Africa ~ After leaving school, Roald Dahl was desperate for adventure. He wanted to see lions and elephants, giraffes and deadly snakes. He wanted to see coconuts and silvery beaches. So he got a job in Africa. In 1938, he began a long journey to the faraway continent. It would be three thrilling years before he returned home. Find out more in **Going Solo**.

Alfhild ~ Alf was Roald Dahl's big sister. She was a genuine eccentric. Here are some of the unusual things she did: she smoked cigars, drank champagne out of her shoe, and danced on tabletops! Roald and Alf were very close—they shared a passion for gardening and gossiped endlessly on the phone. (See Family Tree.)

All done! ~ Once Roald Dahl had finished writing a book, it was time for Wendy Kress, his trusty typist, to turn the pile of yellow scribbled paper into a neat, printed manuscript. Roald wouldn't let anyone disturb Wendy until the book was done. And as she neared the final page, he would pace to and fro, impatient to see the finished work. Then he would worry that he wouldn't have a good enough idea for the next book.

Alma ~ She was the Dahls' pet goat, who lived in the fields at their home, Gipsy House. She once broke into Roald's writing hut and left him a present on the floor (and we're not talking chocolates or flowers!).

Antiques ~ Roald Dahl liked old, precious things and enjoyed poking and rummaging around in antique shops. He opened his own antique shop in Great Missenden for his daughter Tessa, called the Witchball. Later, he owned an antique business called Dahl & Son, which he ran with his son. If you were to stroll down Great Missenden High Street now, you'd see it's become a beauty parlor.

The Apple ~ This was Roald Dahl's nickname at home. He was the only boy of five children and the apple of his mother's eye—that is to say, her favorite.

Art ~ Roald Dahl loved art. He loved learning about it, buying it, and selling it, but most of all, he loved looking at it. If a picture caught his eye, he would snap it up—even if it was far too expensive. . . . Then he'd sometimes have to sell it again when he ran out of money! One of the best things about making it as an author was that he could afford to keep his pictures.

Asta ~ Roald Dahl's youngest sister couldn't wait to fly up, up, and away in the Second World War. She joined the women's branch of the Royal Air Force (the Women's Auxiliary Air Force) and soon became an officer. She flew in barrage balloons in the UK and later commanded a WAAF unit in Norway and even received a medal from Norway's king. (See Family Tree.)

ASTA   ELSE   ALFHILD   ROALD

Astri ~ Tragically, Roald Dahl's eldest sister died from appendicitis when she was just seven years old and Roald was only three. Seven is the same age at which Roald's daughter Olivia died. Today, appendicitis can be easily cured, but in 1920 it was often fatal. (See Family Tree.)

Random Roald Fact

He loved collecting facts. Here's one of
Roald Dahl's favorites—saffron (made from
the stigmas of the purple crocus) is
the most expensive food in the world
when sold by weight.

Attention all writers! ~ Roald Dahl believed a story
should grab its reader from the first sentence. He thought writers need a
lively imagination, stamina (few people get it right first time, unless of
course they're Charles Dickens, but he was a genius and they're rare!),
and, most important of all, a keen sense of humor. It took Roald almost a
year to write each of his children's books.

Autobiography ~ Roald Dahl absolutely, positively, definitely did
not write any autobiographies. He thought they were full of boring
details about a person's life. However, he did write **Boy** and **Going
Solo**—two books that are filled to the brim with bizarre, frightening,
exciting, and funny things that happened to him when he was young.

Aviary ~ Gipsy House was home not just to the Dahl family but also to a hundred homing budgerigars. The birds lived in an amazing aviary that was guarded by two extremely scary eagles. (OK, so they were made of stone, but they were still scary.) Roald's first wife picked up the rocky predators (strong lady!) from a film set in America. They were sent back to England as a present for their son, Theo. Not a single budgie lives in the aviary today, but the eagles stuck around.

bumplehammers
buzzburger
buckswashling

bogthumper
bellypopper
bogglebox

B is for . . .

Baaa! ~ Tessa Dahl once surprised her father by arriving home with two white, fluffy lambs that she'd bought with her pocket money while staying with a friend in the country. But the frisky lambs ate everything in the garden at Gipsy House! In despair, Tessa and Roald had to sneak them into a local farmer's field in the dead of night, hoping they wouldn't be noticed among the other sheep.

> "That chap's going to be a bit puzzled the next time he counts his sheep."
> —ROALD DAHL

Backpack ~ When he was seventeen, Roald Dahl braved the desolate wastes of Newfoundland with the Public Schools Exploring Society. Led by a real, true-life explorer—who had traveled with Captain Scott in Antarctica—fifty fearless fellows trudged for three weeks, surviving on pemmican (a pressed cake of meat, fat, and berries), wild bilberries, boiled lichen, and reindeer moss. They were loaded down by enormous backpacks.

Bacon ~ Roald Dahl loved the smell of bacon sizzling in a frying pan. He even had his own bacon slicer, so that he could carve slices that were exactly right—as thin as tissue paper.

Beards ~ Roald Dahl hated beards. He never grew one and couldn't see why a man would want to hide his face behind a beard. He came to the conclusion that beards were grown to conceal something dreadful in a person's personality. He thought that beards were disgusting and dirty and that they always had food caught up in them. Mr. Twit was one of the foulest and smelliest characters in all of Roald's books—and what did he have stuck to his face? A bristly, nailbrushy beard, of course.

Bedtime stories ~ Roald Dahl often tried out his children's stories on his own children at bedtime. He was a brilliant storyteller and he would transport them to his own make-believe world.

The BFG ~ Roald Dahl first told a version of this story to his children at bedtime. Later, in **Danny the Champion of the World**, Danny's father told the story of **The BFG** at bedtime. After another ten years, Roald finally decided to write the story of the Big Friendly Giant as a proper book. There were certain similarities between Roald's friend and builder, Wally Saunders, and the BFG. Wally had big ears and huge hands ... but Roald never revealed if his friend liked to whizzpop! It was **The BFG** that first brought Roald and Quentin Blake face to face—

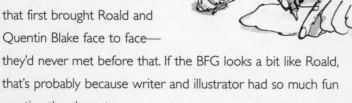

they'd never met before that. If the BFG looks a bit like Roald, that's probably because writer and illustrator had so much fun creating the characters.

Big nostrils ~ This is one way of spotting a real live witch. Witches have extra-big nostrils, especially designed to sniff out children. And witches *hate* children.

Biscuits ~ Roald Dahl tasted the best biscuits in the world at a book-signing session in the Dutch town of Arnhem. The line was so long that the owner of a local patisserie sent over a box of his special biscuits (Arnhemse Meisjes) to keep him going. While Roald's right hand was signing, his left kept sneaking into the box for more of the delicious treats. Roald took the recipe from the baker and he used to make them at home in Gipsy House. If you're ever in Arnhem, look for the Patisserie Hagdorn and taste them for yourself.

" Simply marvelous! "
– ROALD DAHL

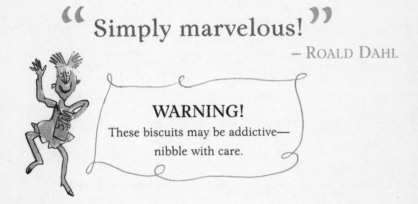

WARNING!
These biscuits may be addictive—
nibble with care.

Blabbermouth ~ Roald Dahl loved secrets but was terrible at keeping them—he was much too fond of talking.

Random Roald Fact
He could speak Swahili.

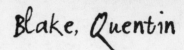

Blake, Quentin

Roald Dahl's stories go hand in hand with Quentin Blake's illustrations—they are a perfect pairing. Quentin first had a drawing published when he was still at school, in **Punch** magazine. He has always made a living as an illustrator, as well as teaching for over twenty years at the Royal College of Art. A hugely successful illustrator, Quentin was chosen to be the first-ever Children's Laureate of Great Britain in 1999.

> "[He's] a national institution."
>
> – *GUARDIAN*

> "Blake is beyond brilliant."
>
> – *DAILY TELEGRAPH*

Quent ~ Roald Dahl's nickname for his favorite illustrator.

> "The finest illustrator of children's books in the world today!"
>
> —ROALD DAHL

Illustrations ~ At the beginning of Roald Dahl's writing career, many illustrators worked on his books. It was not until his editor suggested Quentin Blake, in the late 1970s, that his books got the illustrations they really needed. The two worked together until Roald's death, and since then many new editions of the stories have been published with Quentin's illustrations.

"It is Quent's pictures rather than my own written descriptions that have brought to life such characters as The BFG, Miss Trunchbull, Mr. Twit, and The Grand High Witch."

—ROALD DAHL

"I could never guess what he was going to think of next."

–QUENTIN BLAKE

Little and Large ~ Roald Dahl and Quentin Blake were an unlikely-looking pair, with Roald tall and chatty and Quentin small and quiet, but they got on like a house on fire. It was as they worked on **The BFG** that they became best friends. Roald even encouraged Quentin to take up driving. When a new story was ready, Roald would say things like "You'll have some fun with this," or "You'll have some trouble with this," but Quentin knew absolutely nothing about any story until the manuscript arrived. Then he would produce rough drawings and visit Gipsy House to discuss them. Roald liked his books to be packed with illustrations, and for **The BFG**, Quentin had to produce twice as many pictures as originally planned.

Awards ~ Quentin Blake must need a really long shelf for all the awards he's been given. He's won the Silver Brush Award, the Kurt Maschler Award, the Hans Christian Andersen Award for Illustration, the *New York Times* Best Illustrated Book of the Year, and the Children's Book Award, among others. The queen of England recognized him by naming him an Officer of the Order of the British Empire in 1988.

Blue spit ~ Witches' spit is blue. Look out for the faint blue tinge on their teeth and gums—then run!

Boarding school ~ Roald Dahl was packed off to St. Peter's Boarding School in Weston-super-Mare when he was just nine years old. He hated it and was very homesick. Once he was so desperate to go home that he faked appendicitis. But his plan was rumbled and he was sent back to school.

Boazers ~ The name for prefects at Repton School, where Roald Dahl went to secondary school. These older boys were allowed to boss the younger ones around mercilessly. They could even cane them!

Bogtrotter, Bruce ~ Could you eat an entire chocolate cake in one go like **Matilda**'s chocolate champion, BB? Roald Dahl couldn't. If you offered him some chocolate cake, he wouldn't eat it, as he didn't like chocolate-flavored things, only *real* chocolate.

Bond, James Bond ~ Shhhhh.... Is anyone reading over your shoulder? No? Good. There's a top-secret reason why Roald Dahl was exactly the right person to write the screenplay for the James Bond film **You Only Live Twice**. During the 1940s, in Washington, he worked for the British intelligence service on top-secret stuff. We could tell you more . . . but then we'd have to chop you up into little pieces. Only joking!

Bone and gristle ~ Roald Dahl kept some rather grisly ornaments on the table in his writing hut. There were parts of his own hip joint—the doctor said the hip bone was the biggest he had ever seen. He also kept a glass bottle full of mauve-colored lumps of gristle in a special preserving liquid—a present from his surgeon. Yuck!

Bonfire ~ Roald Dahl worked very hard at making sure every word he wrote was just right. For every page he was happy with, three or four more pages were thrown away. Once a month—when his large wastebasket was full to overflowing with discarded, scribbled-on, yellow pages—Roald made a bonfire just outside his writing shed. (One of the shed's white walls was soon streaked with black.) But not everything went up in smoke. Roald hoarded masses of pieces of paper covered with scribbles and ideas.

Bookworm ~ Roald Dahl's own favorite stories as a child were **The Secret Garden** by Frances Hodgson Burnett, **Swallows and Amazons** by Arthur Ransome, and **Mr. Midshipman Easy** by Captain Frederick Marryat. He also liked Ernest Hemingway and C. S. Forester as he got older.

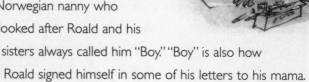

Boy ~ This book describes the nice and nasty things that happened to Roald Dahl when he was young. The Norwegian nanny who looked after Roald and his sisters always called him "Boy." "Boy" is also how Roald signed himself in some of his letters to his mama.

Broccoli, Cubby (Albert R.) ~ Part-owner of the rights for the James Bond films, he said his ancestors invented a curly green vegetable that they christened with their surname—can you guess the vegetable?! They did this by crossing cauliflower with rabe. Cubby worked closely with Roald Dahl when he wrote the screenplay for **You Only Live Twice**. There's one big similarity between the plot of the film and the storyline of **Charlie and the Great Glass Elevator**. If you ever watch the movie, keep your eyes peeled . . . but you won't see James Bond tackling any Vermicious Knids.

Bucket ~ A round, open vessel for carrying water. (Ooops! Almost forgot—Bucket is the name of one of the most important families in the history of books featuring boys called Charlie and lots of chocolate.)

Bugs ~ Roald Dahl became quite an expert on creepy-crawlies when he was planning **James and the Giant Peach**. Did you know, for example, that some bees have tongues that they can unroll until they are twice as long as the bee itself?

Bullies ~ Roald Dahl hated bullies. So when his daughter Lucy and her friends were being bullied on the school bus by a girl called Lizzy, he came up with a plan. He wrote a rhyme and told Lucy to teach it to everyone except the bully. They learned the verse and, when Lizzy next picked on a girl on the bus, everyone sang:

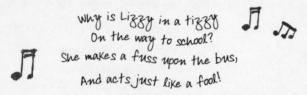

Why is Lizzy in a tizzy
On the way to school?
She makes a fuss upon the bus,
And acts just like a fool!

Everyone on the bus—except Lizzy—cheered, chanted, clapped, and sang over and over again. Lizzy didn't pick on them again. In Roald's books, bullies get their just deserts—see what happens to the aunts in **James and the Giant Peach**, the horrid giants in **The BFG**, and Miss Trunchbull in **Matilda**.

Bursting postbag ~ Roald Dahl received sacks and sacks of mail from fans all over the world—as many as 4,000 letters a week! And he answered every single one of them (with a little help from his secretary and a letter that he adapted each time). Here's one of the letters he wrote:

My teacher wasn't half as nice as yours seems to be.

His name was Mister Unsworth and he taught us history,

And when you didn't know a date he'd get you by the ear

And start to twist while you sat there quite paralyzed with fear.

He'd twist and twist and twist your ear and twist it more and more,

Until at last the ear came off and landed on the floor.

Our class was full of one-eared boys, I'm certain there were eight,

Who'd had them twisted off because they didn't know a date.

So let us now praise teachers who today are all so fine

And yours in particular is totally divine.

Buttercups ~ Roald Dahl's Norwegian grandfather was a naturalist and encouraged young Roald's interest in nature. Roald once ate the bulb of a buttercup and described it as "frighteningly hot." We'll just have to take his word for it.

WARNING!
Do not try eating plants at home!
It's very dangerous to eat anything
growing wild! Always ask an adult!

catasterous

chiddler
cattysiddlers
chatbags

C is for . . .

The Cabin ~ This was the name of the house Roald Dahl's mother used to rent for the Easter holidays in Tenby, Pembrokeshire. It was right next to the sea, and Roald and his sisters used to collect periwinkles and cook them, then eat them on slices of bread and butter. Try this yummy snack for yourself!

Cats ~ Roald Dahl adored dogs, birds, and even goats. But he hated cats.

Cave drawing ~ Roald Dahl as an adult didn't think much of wallpaper. He once announced that he was going to try his hand at cave drawing. He insisted he needed to be alone to be inspired, and single-handedly decorated a whole wall of the house. His family was stunned by the results—until a few weeks later, when his wife, clearing out some drawers, found the stencils he had used to produce his "original" works of art!

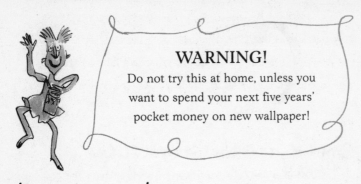

WARNING!

Do not try this at home, unless you
want to spend your next five years'
pocket money on new wallpaper!

Characters with no name ~ No matter how many
times you read **The Witches** or **The Magic Finger**, you never find out
the names of the boy and girl at the heart of these stories, and yet
you feel as if you know them as well as one of your friends.
Discover for yourself. . . .

**Charlie and the
Chocolate Factory ~**
When he'd finished writing this
book, Roald Dahl gave it to his
nephew Nicholas to read. The
surprising verdict was
"rotten and boring," so Roald
took action at once. He rewrote the book,
getting rid of lots of characters while
changing and improving the story.

The original Charlie was just one of fifteen horrible children—not very important at all—and the story was called **Charlie's Chocolate Boy**. Even the visit to the chocolate factory wasn't that special—there was one every Saturday.

Charlie and the Great Glass Elevator

~ A lot of frowning and umming and aaahing went into the title of the sequel to **Charlie and the Chocolate Factory**. At first, Roald Dahl thought the word "elevator" was too American, but the British "lift" seemed far too boring. "Air machine" was considered, but "elevator" came out on top in the end. ("Lift" was used in the text of **Charlie and the Chocolate Factory**.)

Charlie in the . . .

~ Roald Dahl began writing a third story about Charlie Bucket (**Charlie in the White House**) but sadly only left a tantalizing first chapter. Here's a little snippet. Can you think up what happened next?

Charlie = the White House   *Roald Dahl*

The President of the United States was standing on
the lawn of The White House. He was surrounded by all the
most important people in the country. They were wearing
their best clothes and there was an air of tremendous
excitement everywhere. The President himself was gazing
anxiously at the sky. He was searching for the helicopter
which was due to arrive at any minute. This helicopter,
as everyone knew, was bringing to The White House the eight
brave astronauts who only a few hours before had rescued
an American spaceship when it was attacked by a swarm of
Vermicious Knids.

So, standing on the lawn were:

The President of the United States, Lancelot R. Gilligrass,
the most powerful man on earth.

The Vice-President, Miss Tibbs, a gigantic and fearsome
lady of eighty-nine who had been the President's nanny
when he was small.

Then we had the President's Inner Cabinet. This
consisted of five men. They were the President's closest
advisers and they were all immensely powerful. Together
with the President and the Vice-President, these five men
ran the country. They were:

The Chief of the Army, General Horsebrass, who was
wearing so many medal-ribbons they covered not only the front
and back of his tunic but ran all the way down his pants as well.

The Chief of the Navy, Admiral Tarbuncle, who was all at
sea on land.

The Director of Sewage and Garbage Disposal, the Honourable
I. M. Ponky, who was standing all by himself because nobody
wanted to come too close to him, even downwind.

The Director of Public Relations and Bamboozlement,
Wilbur G. Pocus, known as Hocus to his friends.

The Co-ordinator of Hi-Fi and Hearing Aids, Mr. Bugsy Tape,
who was hiding in a hollow tree and recording every word that
was spoken on The White House lawn.

There were lots of other famous and important people
there, but there isn't room to mention them all.

Chart topper ~ Charlie and the Chocolate Factory set a record: the Chinese print run was 2 million copies, the biggest of any book at the time! Roald Dahl's books have sold over 90 million copies worldwide, and more than 2 million copies of **Charlie and the Chocolate Factory** have sold in the U.S. alone

The Child Catcher ~ Roald Dahl co-wrote the screenplay for the film version of Ian Fleming's **Chitty Chitty Bang Bang**. He thought up the cruellest, most cunning, most conniving character in the entire film—the evil Child Catcher.

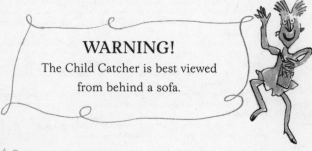

WARNING!
The Child Catcher is best viewed
from behind a sofa.

crumpscoddle
chiddler
catasterous

Children's Book Award ~ In 1989, **Matilda** won the prestigious Red House Children's Book Award. Roald Dahl was over the moon, because the judges weren't stuffy old grown-up critics—they were everyday kids!

The Chilterns ~ Roald Dahl loved the countryside around Gipsy House, and he used it as the setting for **Fantastic Mr. Fox** and **Danny the Champion of the World**. The movie of Danny was even filmed in the Chilterns. Part of **Chitty Chitty Bang Bang** was filmed near Roald's house, too.

Random Roald Fact
He liked children better than adults
and ladies better than gents.

CHOCOLATE FACTS

Cadbury ~ Roald Dahl and his school friends were very lucky. They were sometimes asked by Cadbury—the chocolate manufacturer—to test newly invented chocolate bars. Roald used to dream of inventing a world-famous chocolate bar that would win the praise of the great Mr. Cadbury himself.

Chocoholic ~ Roald Dahl was a total chocoholic. He absolutely adored the stuff.

After-dinner chocolate ~ If you were invited to dinner at Roald Dahl's house, at the end of the meal, you'd be offered a red plastic box containing all of Roald's favorite chocolates—Twix, Kit Kats, Rolos, Smarties, Flakes, and Maltesers. When he was an adult, Roald also used to buy fancy chocolates from a shop in London.

"Gloriumptious!"
—ROALD DAHL

Seven glorious years ~ Roald Dahl believed that the greatest chocolate bars and chocolates ever were invented during the seven glorious years from 1930 to 1937. This was the time of the Aero, Black Magic, Crunchies, Kit Kats, Maltesers, Mars bars, Quality Street, Rolos, and Smarties.

Dead Ducks ~ The disasters of the chocolate world in Roald Dahl's opinion were the Double Decker and the Cadbury's Creme Egg.

Energy Balls ~ In 1936, Forrest Mars, son of the founder of Mars, worked hard to think up a new chocolate sensation. He took a pea-sized piece of dough flavored with malted milk, exploded it in a vacuum, and covered it with melted chocolate. Hey, presto—the Energy Ball, quickly renamed the Malteser (or the Malted Milk Ball), was born!

Hot chocolate fact ~ Did you know that chocolate was first used in Spain, Italy, France, and England in the seventeenth century—but only as a drink? It was another one hundred years before a Swiss man made a real milk chocolate bar. Thank goodness he did.

History ~ Roald Dahl thought that dry, crusty dates like 1066 (the Battle of Hastings) were of no use whatsoever to a child. He believed instead, that kids should be taught mouthwatering dates such as:

1932—the first production of the Mars bar
1936—the first production of Maltesers
1937—the birth of the Kit Kat and Rolos
1938—the birth of Smarties

"If I were a headmaster, I would get rid of the history teacher and get a chocolate teacher instead. . . ."

—ROALD DAHL

Chopper ~ Roald Dahl's
much-loved brown and white Jack
Russell terrier, Chopper, who was very
naughty, was the last dog he owned.
Chopper was fed on a diet of
oysters, caviar, Smarties, and the
occasional can of dog food. He
used to accompany Roald
everywhere—they even
appeared on TV together—and
he always seemed to know what

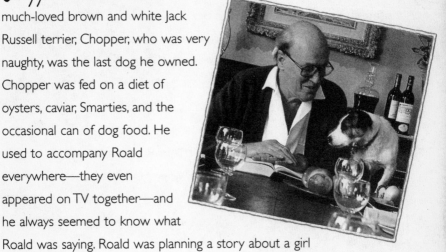

Roald was saying. Roald was planning a story about a girl
and a dog who understood each other's language when he died. Only
three members of Roald's family ever appeared in his books: his
granddaughter Sophie in **The BFG**; Chopper in **Matilda**, although as a
parrot; and Alma the goat in **George's Marvellous Medicine**. Chopper
lived to the ripe old age of sixteen—not bad for a little dog.

Christmas ~ Roald Dahl loved Christmas as a child but loathed it
as an adult. He thought that it forced people to spend too much money
on presents they couldn't afford and therefore took the magic away. He
believed the best presents were the simplest ones—like the glass jar of
wine gums given to him by his daughter Ophelia.

Clippings ~ Roald Dahl clipped these pictures of mouths and eyes out of newspapers and magazines to give him inspiration for new characters. What type of people do the clippings conjure up in your mind?

Comfort ~ Roald Dahl could only work when he was totally comfortable. His writing hut was full of gadgets. These included a seat with a hole (to prevent pressure on an abcess that had formed on the base of his spine), a writing board of exactly the right thickness, tilted at exactly the right angle, and an old suitcase filled with logs for a footrest. His legs were tucked up in a green sleeping bag. He also rigged up a rickety old space heater on two parallel wires on the ceiling and would pull it toward him when he got cold—definitely not an invention to try out yourself!

Comics ~ Roald Dahl loved reading. At boarding school, he was always desperate for the parcel from home—it was bound to contain new comics. He especially liked one called **Bubbles**.

Concoctions ~ Roald Dahl mixed the strangest ingredients together to create teatime treats for his children, like delicious bacon and marmalade sandwiches. As he placed the treat on the table he would casually say, "This is a secret recipe. A young prince in Dar es Salaam passed it on to me after I saved him from the dreadful grip of a giant python." Then he made them swear that they would never give the recipes away and sauntered off back to his writing hut in the garden.

"Could do better" ~ As a best-selling children's author (and rule bender!), Roald Dahl was keen to help out his daughter Lucy with her English homework. He wrote a story especially for her, then Lucy copied it out neatly and handed it in. Both she and her dad were horrified when the teacher returned it marked: "C—you could do better."

> **Random Roald Fact**
> His favorite color was yellow.

Crafty conker tips ~

Conker champion Roald Dahl's best-ever conker was his 109—it was called this because it had survived 109 hard-fought conker contests. Roald was always experimenting with different ways to make a chestnut into the unbreakable, unsmashable, ultimate conker. He tried soaking them in vinegar and baking them in the oven, but nothing seemed to work better than the slow, classic and not-very-instant method of storing conkers in a dry place for a whole year.

Creamy Kit Kat pudding ~

Put a layer of Kit Kats in the bottom of a dish. Then a layer of whipped cream. Then a layer of Kit Kats. Then another of whipped cream and so on for as long as you like. Put the whole thing in the freezer. Serve in slices when frozen. Mmmm . . .

Crowds ~
Roald Dahl's fans turned out in huge numbers to see and hear their hero wherever he went. When he visited Amsterdam, in the Netherlands, the crowds were so big that the mounted police were called out to control them.

Curtains ~ Roald Dahl loved to escape to his hut in the garden, where he would draw the curtains to make sure he was really alone. Soon it became the only place he wanted to be when he was writing. His family knew never to disturb him there, but cows grazing outside in the orchard didn't. They sometimes licked the windows and tried to nibble the curtains!

"It's marvelous, isolated, quiet."
—ROALD DAHL

Cushions ~ As a child, Roald Dahl used to tie cushions around his sisters so that he could fire his toy gun at them!

D is for . . .

Dahl, Roald ~ It's pronounced 'Roo-ahl' in Norwegian—you must have heard of him! See below:

Autograph	*Roald Dahl*
Birthday	13 September, 1916
Color of eyes	Blue-grey
Color of hair	Greyish
Special virtue	Never satisfied with what I've done.
Special vice	Drinking
Favorite color	Yellow
Favorite food	Caviar

Favorite music　　　Beethoven

Favorite personality　　　My wife and children

Favorite sound　　　Piano

Favorite TV program　　　News

Favorite smell　　　Bacon frying

Favorite book when young　　　"Mr. Midshipman Easy"

If I wasn't an author I'd like to be　　A Doctor

My most frightening moment　　In a Hurricane, 1941, RAF

My funniest moment　　Being born

Motto

My candle burns at both ends
It will not last the night
But ah my foes and oh my friends
It gives a lovely light.

Dahl's Chickens
~ Can you work out which famous Victorian author the BFG meant when he said this?

Dahl's day
~ Roald Dahl had a very strict daily routine. He would eat breakfast in bed and open his mail. When ideas were flowing, he worked in his writing hut from 10:30 A.M. till 12 P.M. and from 4 P.M. till 6 P.M. His typical lunch would be a gin and tonic followed by Norwegian prawns with mayonnaise and lettuce and a Kit Kat for dessert. After a snooze, and armed with a Thermos flask of tea, he returned to the Hut to work. He would be back at the house at six o'clock on the dot, ready for his dinner.

Danny the Champion of the World
~ This book started life as an adult story—called "The Champion of the World"—and slowly grew into one of Roald Dahl's most popular children's novels. It is set in Great Missenden and bears the closest resemblance to Roald's own environment of all his books.

Dedications ~ Roald Dahl always dedicated his books to special people in his life—mostly members of his family. Who would you dedicate a book to?

Desert trek ~ During the Second World War, Roald Dahl served with the Royal Air Force in the Middle East. Eager to explore, he and three friends drove for hours, far across the Iraqi desert, to the ancient ghost town of Babylon—a city so old that it is mentioned in the Bible. It is a place of mystery, deserted and silent, with streets and houses about 66 feet below ground level and lions and mythical beasts carved into the city's sandy walls.

De Vito, Danny ~ A huge fan of Roald Dahl's, the director of **Matilda** (1996), Danny De Vito, wanted to make sure that the film was perfect. So, every day, he listened to a recording of Roald reading **Fantastic Mr. Fox** as he drove to the studio. This made him feel closer to the great writer.

Dhal ~ A spicy Indian dish made from lentils. Ooops, sorry—wrong type of Dahl.

Random Roald Fact

He played a game of snooker with the former world champion Cliff Thorburn. Thorburn autographed the wall of Roald's snooker room.

Dirty Beasts ~ This is a wickedly funny collection of verses by Roald Dahl about some outrageous animals. Below is an extract from a poem called "The Porcupine," where a young girl sits on a porcupine, gets its spikes stuck in her bottom, and dashes to the dentist for help!

"Quite honestly I can't pretend
I've ever pulled things from this end."
He started pulling one by one
And yelling "My, oh my, what fun!"
I shouted "Help!" I shouted "Ow!"
He said, "It's nearly over now."

You'll have to find a copy of the book to discover what happens next!

Doctors ~ Roald Dahl was no stranger to
the doctor's scalpel. He was regularly fixed up by
doctors. He thought they did a marvelous job
and secretly longed to be a doctor himself
(although he adored being a writer).

Dogs' droppings ~ To a witch, the
smell of a child is exactly like the smell of
dogs' droppings. The cleanest children smell
worst of all.

Door handles ~ In the Roald Dahl Children's Gallery at the
Buckinghamshire County Museum, the door handles are really hip.
Sorry . . . they're really hips! The handles are modeled on Roald's actual
replacement hip (or "metal prosthesis," to be properly medical about it).
He used to use his metal hip to hook open his filing cabinet drawers
when he was sitting in the Hut. In case you are confused, this "spare" hip
was from his first operation—it had to be replaced again, because he
sprang out of bed before it was ready.

Random Roald Fact

Roald once put his first wife's coat in
the freezer to store it through the
summer. Pat was horrified but the
coat was pretty chilled out!

Dream blower ~ Sometimes, when he was feeling particularly mischievous, Roald Dahl would prop a ladder against the side of his house, climb up to the bedroom windows—just as his children were drifting off to sleep—and push a bamboo cane through their window, pretending to be the BFG.

Dreams ~ Roald Dahl slept for only three or four hours a night, but he crammed these hours full of dreams. One of his top-ten dreams starred himself as a tramp arriving at Lord's Cricket Ground with a shabby case containing a million pounds. He told the English cricketers that if he played on their team, they would beat the Aussies. If the team lost, he would hand over his million pounds. Roald was always the last batsman, leading the side to victory. His dream usually ended with him and the team being driven around the country in an open-top bus, hailed by all as heroes . . . but of course, it was only a dream.

Dust ~ Roald Dahl's writing hut was *never* dusted. Just like Willy Wonka's inventing room, it was a top-secret place. Roald wouldn't allow anyone inside, even to clean it, and so it remained full of grime and spiderwebs, but sparkling with ideas!

doddleflap

disgustable

duckhound

dibbler

delumptious

dadsy

dogswoggler

E is for . . .

extrausual
exunctly
eyebones
elefunt

Easter-egg hunt ~ Roald Dahl loved Easter, especially the eggstraordinarily eggciting and eggstremely eggstravagant egg hunts he went on as a child.

Ellen ~ Roald Dahl used to refer to Ellen as his ancient half-sister, because she was twelve years older than he. After Roald returned home from the Second World War, with no idea whether his family was dead or alive, his ancient half-sister Ellen was the very first person he managed to make contact with, because Roald knew her married name, and she and her husband were in the phone book. She put him in touch with his mother and other sisters, who had moved to Aylesbury, England. Hurrah! (See Family Tree.)

Else ~ Roald Dahl's middle sister hated school. When her mother decided to send her to boarding school in Switzerland, she devised a foolproof plan. She ate her train ticket at the Gare du Nord station in Paris and had to be collected and brought home! Roald loved Else very much. (See Family Tree.)

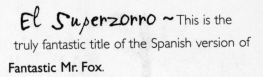

El Superzorro ~ This is the truly fantastic title of the Spanish version of **Fantastic Mr. Fox.**

Endings ~ Of all Roald Dahl's books, the most talked-about ending belongs to **The Witches.** (It's hard to believe, but there might—just might—be one or two Dahl fans on earth who have yet to finish this wonderfully wicked book, so . . . you won't find the actual ending here.) Roald was horrified to find out that in the film version of **The Witches** his quirky ending had been changed. He threatened to remove his name from the credits in protest. What do you think of the real ending? In some of Roald's endings you discover that the main character in the story is a writer too and their book is the one you have just read—for example, **The BFG** and **James and the Giant Peach.**

> ## Random Roald Fact
> He once filled his ancient
> half-sister's fiancé's pipe
> with goat droppings.

E is for *The Enormous Crocodile*

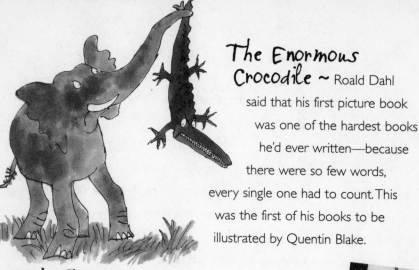

The Enormous Crocodile ~ Roald Dahl

said that his first picture book was one of the hardest books he'd ever written—because there were so few words, every single one had to count. This was the first of his books to be illustrated by Quentin Blake.

Esio Trot ~ The rather topsy-turvy title for this

story is actually the word "tortoise" spelled backward. Aedi citsatnaf!

Essays ~ Roald Dahl's book of essays—written in

1927 when he was eleven—is still in one piece. If you want to find out what the young Roald had to say about "Summer Holidays," "Gardening," "The Life Story of a Penny," and "It's Better to Play a Game and Lose than Never to Play at All," you can read his essays at the Roald Dahl Museum and Story Centre in Great Missenden, England.

fizzwinkle

fizzwiggler

fibster

F is for . . .

frobscottle

foulsome

flubboxed

Fairies ~ If you ever visited Roald Dahl's home in Great Missenden, you might have noticed some strange goings-on in the garden. If you looked carefully on the lawn, you would perhaps have seen the word "Hello!" written in yellow letters. Roald would have told you that this was a message from the fairies. In actual fact, it was one of his little tricks—he did this from time to time, writing the words in weedkiller when no one was looking. His daughters Ophelia and Lucy loved to see their names written on the lawn in fairy writing.

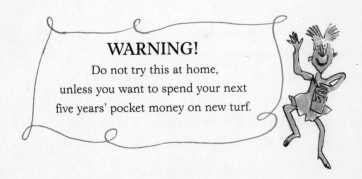

WARNING!
Do not try this at home,
unless you want to spend your next
five years' pocket money on new turf.

Fantastic Mr. Fox ~ Roald Dahl first wrote this as a picture book called **Mr. Fox**. But as the story grew and grew, it became more and more fantastic. The book was renamed **Fantastic Mr. Fox** a matter of days before it went to print.

Feathered friends ~ Roald Dahl owned a hundred homing budgerigars—yellow ones, green ones, blue ones, and white ones. He also had a mynah bird that had been taught to say very rude things, like "*!*%!" (You didn't think we'd print them in this book, did you?) If you repeat those words, you might end up like the mynah bird in **Matilda**, which was given away! Roald hated people shooting birds for sport—you can see this best in **The Magic Finger**.

Fighter pilot ~ During the Second World War, Roald Dahl flew several planes, including Hurricanes, Tiger Moths, and Gladiators, on dangerous and nerve-racking missions. After just eight

weeks' training with the Royal Air Force, Roald could fly upside down and get out of a dangerous spin—on his own. He was extraordinarily lucky to survive. Delve into **Going Solo** to find out more about his daring escapades.

Film critic ~ Although Roald Dahl wrote the screenplay for **Willy Wonka and the Chocolate Factory** (1971), he never liked the actual film. It was a box office success, though, so you'll have to make up your own mind.

First-class letter-writers ~ Roald Dahl received more sacks of mail from Australia than from anywhere else in the world. But he only ever visited the country once, in 1989.

First ever story ~ During the Christmas holidays when Roald Dahl was ten, he wrote his first short story, "Kumbak II," about a newly invented machine that could tune in to conversations from the past.

The "Kumbak II."

the other day I went to stay with my uncle Aristotle, who was a young and particulary leaned man, who was keen on wireless, and all all such inventions.

Mary, the housekeeper, told me that he had been rather irritable lately, and that I would be wise if I did not disturbe him at all, but left him completly alone to his studies.

My first evening he came out of his room, which Mary called his "wireness room," and greeted me cheerily. He looked about 30 and he was lean and small, but with rosy cheeks, and I noticed with joy that he seemed very pleased with him self.

The following day I spent in exploring the garden, at least I pretended that I was doing so, by in reality I was trying to peep into the wireness room, I overheard, and eventually suceeded partially for the window was covered with a green curtain, But at the top it had a tiny gape, where several wires passed out of the window; some to the roof, some to the ground and somealong the side of the house, the latter which I followed, went completly round the house once, being nailed to the brick wall no doubt some new kind of ariel I thought.

But all the morning I silently .... it was going on eventualy I got fed up with .... the steps were 4 high enough, and old Crumers .... din't give me the ladder, so I sat down and thought eventually, I thought of a new idea, so I went up to my room took the mirror that

Fishing ~ On family summer holidays in Norway, Roald Dahl and his sisters would row out into the fjord and drop their fishing lines, baited with mussels. Then they had to sit still in total silence in case the fish heard them and swam away. This was a big challenge for Roald, who always had lots to say. When he hooked a fish he'd shout, "I've got a whopper!" Once they'd caught enough, they'd row back to their mother, who fried the fish gently in butter and served it with boiled potatoes.

"I have never tasted fish as good."

—ROALD DAHL

Fishmonger ~ Never mind the fishy smell, this was Roald Dahl's favorite type of shop. On his seventieth birthday, a fisherman's slab was set up in a marquee in the garden. As well as colorful, shiny fish of all sorts, there were fish and shell sculptures carved out of ice.

Fleming, Ian ~ Roald Dahl and the author of the James Bond books met in Jamaica and New York, through a mutual friend, and became good friends. They had lots in common—including their top-secret intelligence work during the 1940s (Fleming worked for the British Naval intelligence division). Roald wrote the screenplay for the Bond film **You Only Live Twice** and co-wrote the screenplay for Fleming's **Chitty Chitty Bang Bang**.

Flood! ~ While training in the Royal Air Force during the Second World War, Roald Dahl spent time in Iraq. When the great river Euphrates burst its banks, he was on sandbag duty, desperately trying to save people's homes from the rapidly rising water.

Flying ~ Roald Dahl learned to fly when he served in the Royal Air Force during the Second World War. He was far too tall (just over 6 ½ feet) for lots of the planes he flew, spending many hours with his knees touching his chin—but loving every minute of it. It's little wonder that many of his books feature flying: James in his giant peach, Charlie in Mr. Wonka's elevator and Billy aboard a swan in **The Minpins**.

Football ~ Roald Dahl supported Cardiff City Football Club. When he was young, the highlight of his Saturday was going to watch the match with Jones, the family's football-mad gardener. Football is called "soccer" in the U.S.

Footprints ~ In the church-yard at Great Missenden, big, friendly, giant footprints lead to Roald Dahl's grave.

France ~ This is where Roald Dahl spent his first holiday alone, when he was sixteen. He set out with a small suitcase, a large helping of curiosity and twenty-four pounds (about $125 in those days) in his pocket. He saw his first-ever palm trees in Marseilles and spent the next ten days exploring before heading back home. By the time he reached Dover he didn't have a penny left, so he plucked up the courage to ask a kind-looking gentleman if he could borrow a few shillings. The man gave him a ten-shilling note as a present. Roald never forgot this kindness.

Free fruit ~ When Roald Dahl moved into Gipsy House, there were seventy old fruit trees in the orchard—apples, pears, plums, and cherries. There was so much fruit that the children in the village were invited to call in, borrow a ladder, and pick as much as they wanted.

Freezer ~ Roald Dahl invented an ingenious method of stretching shoes, so that they were more comfortable. If your shoes are too tight, fill plastic bags with water, put the bags in the shoes and the shoes in the freezer. The bags get bigger as ice forms and the shoes s-t-r-e-t-c-h!

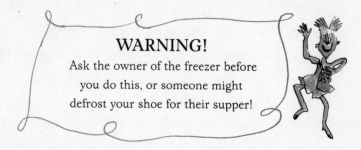

WARNING!
Ask the owner of the freezer before you do this, or someone might defrost your shoe for their supper!

Funeral ~ Roald Dahl died of a form of leukemia in 1990 at the age of seventy-four. His family and friends, and the whole of the book world, were devastated. He was writing up to the very end. His last published book was **The Minpins**. Typically of Roald, he had booked the choir for his funeral while he was still alive and had left instructions for a simple ceremony in his local church, St. Peter and St. Paul. Peter Mayer, the man who was in charge of his publisher, Penguin Books, in 1990, came over from

America to pay tribute to Roald. He began: "Dahl was a very big man. He took up much space. He made us and everyone aware of him." This is how he is remembered—big, not simply in size but as a man, a writer, a father, and a human being.

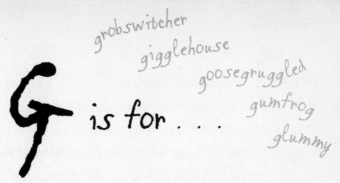

grobswitcher
gigglehouse
goosegruggled
gumfrog
glummy

G is for . . .

Gadgets ~ When the boys at Repton School couldn't afford the latest gadgets, they made them. And we're not talking slingshots here— the resourceful lads made a wireless radio and a phonograph.

Gambling ~ As an adult, Roald Dahl was rather fond of gambling. Together with his friend Claud, he bred and trained racing greyhounds, which had a lucky streak for a while. Claud also taught Roald how to poach pheasants and tickle trout (see **Danny the Champion of the World**). Roald loved the card game Blackjack, too, and horse-racing. In his first job at Shell, he would place a bet on a horse and then sneak out of the office in the afternoon to buy a paper to see if he'd won. He never made his fortune from gambling!

Games ~ Roald Dahl particularly liked chess and Scrabble. He wasn't very good at Scrabble, though, because of his wonky spelling. If you had played with him, you might have smelled a rat as he kept pulling the highest-scoring tiles from the bag. The answer . . . he had learned the feel of the indentations on the high ones!

Gawpers ~ Roald Dahl became so famous that his home was soon well known, too. Uninvited celebrity-spotters often visited, just to see Gipsy House. They stared into the garden, hoping to catch a glimpse of Roald, took pictures, and generally gawped and gazed. Roald didn't really mind. He was pleased to know that people admired him and his books.

George's Marvellous Medicine ~

Roald Dahl found inspiration in all sorts of strange places.

George Kranky's grandma in **George's Marvellous Medicine** had "a small puckered-up mouth like a dog's bottom." So, if you want to know what George's grandma's mouth was like . . . well, you know where to look.

GGG ~ When translated into Italian, the Big Friendly Giant becomes **Il Grande Gigante Gentile**. So, in Italy, the book is called **GGG**!

Giant ~ Roald Dahl was a giant of a man, towering above most people he met. He was just over 6 ½ feet tall. It may have been his great height that made him clumsy. Roald was always knocking things over.

Did You Know?

The world's tallest man was American Robert Wadlow who reached a height of almost 9 feet!

Giant letters ~ Roald Dahl

occasionally wrote letters to schools in BFG style and sent pieces for newsletters as though they really were from the BFG.

Gipsy House ~ In 1954, Roald Dahl became the proud owner of

Little Whitefields—a smallish, square house in Great Missenden, Buckinghamshire. He bought it at auction, without ever having seen it. The house was altered, fixed, and extended, and in 1963 renamed Gipsy House by Roald to avoid confusion with his sister Else's place, Whitefields. He called it Gipsy House because of the Gypsies who lived up the hill. Roald used to take them food, and in return they blessed the house. Roald lived there with his family for the rest of his life.

The Giraffe and the Pelly and Me ~ This book started with just three characters

that Roald Dahl tried out on Quentin Blake. Quentin liked the idea of a giraffe because he'd never drawn one. He knew he could have fun with a pelican's huge

beak. And Roald wanted to include a
monkey because he loved the one Quentin had drawn
in **The Enormous Crocodile**. The characters were
agreed—and the story followed.

Gliders ~ Roald Dahl and his family could often be found
flying model gliders on a hillside near their home. Perhaps this reminded
Roald of swooping and soaring as a fighter pilot in the Second World War.

Gobblefunk A–Z ~ This is a collection of new words Roald Dahl
made up while writing **The BFG** (283 in total). You can see them scattered
around this book, but not all of them made it into the final version.

Going, going, gone! ~ Roald Dahl enjoyed the speed and
excitement of auctions (public sales where an auctioneer accepts higher
and higher bids from the "audience" and bangs his hammer when
something is sold). One of his last books, **The Vicar of Nibbleswicke**, went
under the hammer during an auction that Roald followed eagerly from his
hospital bed. All proceeds were donated to the Dyslexia Institute.

Going Solo ~ This book continues Roald Dahl's story from
where **Boy** left off. It tells of his life in Africa working for Shell, and in the
Royal Air Force in the Second World War. There are stories of deadly

snakes and gentle lions and death-defying dogfights in the
skies above Greece.

golf ~ Roald Dahl first swung a golf club when he was
only nine years old. From then on, he played wherever he
went: Tanganyika, Kenya, Egypt, Sierra Leone, France, America. . . . But this
relaxed game wasn't without danger. In Dar es Salaam, golfers had to
watch out for cobras, and in Lagos, monkeys pelted them with unripe
mangoes!

"One of the loveliest games in the world . . ."

—ROALD DAHL

A grand plan ~ When he was in the hospital once, Roald Dahl
desperately wanted to see his dog Chopper. He came up with a cunning
plan to smuggle him onto the premises (even though animals were
strictly forbidden).

1. Swear family to secrecy.
2. Ask a loyal family member to smuggle a large basket
   into Roald's hospital room.
3. Lower basket out of the window down to the ground—
   five floors below.

4. Instruct another family member to pop Chopper into the basket.
5. Up goes the basket and—ta-daaaa!—Roald spends thirty minutes with his favorite dog.

Sadly, the plan was never tested out because no one could trust Chopper to keep quiet and still!

The Great Automatic Grammatizator and Other Stories ~ This book of short stories

was published in 1996 and contains a selection of Roald Dahl's adult stories from his collected works. Highly recommended for teenage readers. (In the U.S., it's called **The Umbrella Man**.)

The Gremlins ~ You might think **James and the Giant Peach**

was Roald Dahl's first children's book but it wasn't. Long before that he wrote **The Gremlins**. This story first appeared in **Cosmopolitan** magazine in 1942 and it was published as a book the following year, although it is now out of print. It is about "gremlins," mischievous sprites or troublemakers who plagued Royal Air Force pilots. Before he knew it, Roald was being whisked off to Hollywood to work with the great Walt Disney on a movie version of his story. Unfortunately, the film was never completed for various reasons, including its going over budget and because opinion polls showed a drop in interest in war-related topics.

Grown-ups ~ Roald Dahl had vivid memories of his own childhood, of looking up at adults and thinking that they were giants. The character Sophie in **The BFG** showed how it felt to be in the company of giants.

"If you want to remember what it's like to live in a child's world, you've got to get down on your hands and knees and live like that for a week."

—ROALD DAHL

Grrrr! ~ The question Roald Dahl dreaded most was "Where do you get your ideas from?" If he was in a bad mood, he would reply crossly, "Where do you think Beethoven got his from?" But sometimes he would show fans his precious ideas book, where he jotted down thoughts that popped into his head.

Grumpy ~ Roald Dahl tended to get grumpy as he was drawing near the end of a book, and when he'd finished, he felt terrible. He was afraid that he would never be able to write another one. He would sit, moan, scribble away, and just hope that new ideas would pop into his head. They always did. **Matilda** was the only book he felt pleased with once he'd penned the last word.

Gums ~ When Roald Dahl's brother-in-law Leslie Hansen had to have all his teeth out, he absolutely refused to have false ones. From then on, he ate everything—even big, juicy steaks—using his gums.

Did You Know?
Michel Lotito from France can eat just about anything. He has consumed eighteen bicycles, eighteen TV sets, and a Cessna light aircraft, among other things!

Guy Fawkes ~ The best night of
the year at Roald Dahl's first boarding
school was November 5—Bonfire
Night on Guy Fawkes Day. Every
single pupil was given a bag of
fireworks to set off on the football field after dark. Roald joined in this
fireworks ritual for four years and in all that time, amazingly, no one got
seriously hurt.

WARNING!
Don't try this yourself.
Fireworks are very dangerous!

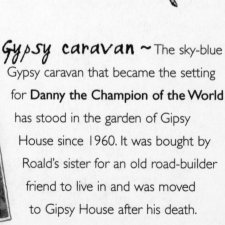

Gypsy caravan ~ The sky-blue
Gypsy caravan that became the setting
for **Danny the Champion of the World**
has stood in the garden of Gipsy
House since 1960. It was bought by
Roald's sister for an old road-builder
friend to live in and was moved
to Gipsy House after his death.

It has survived decapitation—on its journey to Roald's house, the caravan was driven under a very low bridge, slicing the roof clean off—and flames, which were dramatically put out by Roald and his garden hose. Roald's children had great fun playing in it and even camped out in it sometimes.

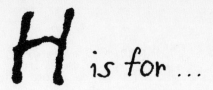

H is for ...

Ha ha ha! ~ Roald Dahl liked to make his readers giggle, guffaw, chuckle, chortle, and explode with laughter. Have you ever read any of his books without making even the teensiest snigger? Bet you haven't!

> **"You can write about anything for children as long as you've got humor."**
> —ROALD DAHL

Hair ~ Roald Dahl didn't like the idea of losing his hair. He even wrote a revolting recipe to make hair grow. And he never visited the barber, preferring instead to have his hair cut at home by his wife's hairdresser. Sadly, he couldn't stop it vanishing in the end!

Did You Know?
The longest hair in the world is almost 17 feet long! The longest ear hair belongs to a man in India and measures 4 inches.

Hard Black Stinker ~ When he was young, Roald Dahl and his family scooted about the Norwegian fjords in a battered old motorboat called the **Hard Black Stinker**. Mama was never afraid to take the helm, whatever the weather. On sunny days, she ferried her family to and from tiny islands, where they picnicked and swam. On stormy days, she bounced the **Hard Black Stinker** from one massive wave to another, while Roald and his sisters clung to the sides, cheering her on.

> **"There was no nonsense about wearing life jackets in those days. We simply clung on to the sides of the boat . . . getting soaked to the skin."**
>
> —ROALD DAHL

Did You Know?
Chinese and Turkish boats often have an eye painted on the side. This is for good luck—and so the boat can see where it is going.

Hard-hitter ~
At school, Roald Dahl was so eager to be a fantastic hockey player that he once secretly wound copper wire around his stick to add weight. He hoped that this would help him to hit the ball farther.

Hemingway, Ernest (1899-1961) ~
This great American writer and Nobel Prize winner (1954) is best known for his novel **A Farewell to Arms**. Roald Dahl and Hemingway were friends and Roald always tried to follow Hemingway's advice: "When you're going good—stop writing."

Hiding places ~
When he was younger, Roald Dahl made sure that his diaries were well hidden . . . so well hidden, in fact, that they have never been found. As an adult, he hid his gambling money, too—under the floorboards. The kind of hiding that Roald loved best of all, however, was shutting himself away in the Hut to think up wonderful stories.

Hooray (and boo) for Hollywood! ~
In the Hollywood Hills of Los Angeles, California—the movie capital of the world—Roald Dahl had some of the best and some of the worst times ever. He loved the excitement of working for Walt Disney and meeting great stars. But he was very upset when his film **The Gremlins** was cancelled. Later, when his first wife became very ill while acting in a Hollywood film, enough was enough. Roald packed his family's bags and returned to England for good.

Hope ~ When Tim Burton approached Roald Dahl's widow about his plan to make a film of **James and the Giant Peach**, she asked him why he wanted to do it. Burton's answer clinched the deal: "It's the only book that ever gave me any hope when I was a child."

Hot-house Eggs ~ Roald Dahl took over the cooking when his first wife was ill, and he tried to be as imaginative with food as he was with words. He served up bright pink milk and transformed plain old fried eggs and fried bread into Hot-house Eggs, which tasted scrumptious and looked superb.

Recipe for Hot-house Eggs
(Be sure to ask an adult for help.)

1. Cut a circle out of a slice of bread.
2. Pop the bread into a buttered pan and cook on both sides.
3. Crack the egg in the hole in the bread.
4. The egg oozes across the bread as it cooks.
5. Mmmm . . .

The Hut ~ Roald Dahl wrote his books in a white hut on the edge of the orchard at Gipsy House. It was an exact copy of the author Dylan Thomas's writing hut, which Roald once visited. He got his friend Wally Saunders to build it—out of bricks and with a yellow front door. It was very cozy, with sheets of polystyrene lining the walls and a dangerous-looking overhead contraption to keep him warm. The Hut still stands exactly as Roald left it, with everything set up ready for writing. His cigarette ends are in the ashtray and the wastebasket is almost full, as if he had just popped out for a bit.

hippodumplings

hullaballoo

huggybee

hushyquiet

horridest

hopscotchy

$\mathbf{I}$ is for ...

icky-poo

Ideas ~ Roald Dahl kept two ideas books for about forty years. They were both old school exercise books, the first of which was sandy colored, and the second red and very battered. He thought that good ideas were like dreams—soon forgotten—and made sure that he wrote them down straight away. He then checked off the really good ideas and crossed out the ones he had used. Some ideas were developed years and years after they were jotted down. Can you guess which books came from these ideas?

A story about Mr. Fox who has a whole network of underground tunnels leading to all the shops in the village. At night, he goes up through the floorboards and helps himself.

Fantastic Mr. Fox

What about a chocolate factory
That makes fantastic and marvellous
Things — with a crazy man running it?

Charlie and the Chocolate Factory

If . . . ~ If Roald Dahl hadn't been an author, he could have been a doctor, a boxer, a golfer, an inventor, a scientist, a botanist, or a picture framer. He had a natural talent for all of these things.

Interests ~ Roald Dahl was interested in just about EVERYTHING. But here are a few of the things he was especially fascinated by:

nineteenth- and twentieth-century paintings
eighteenth-century English furniture
gardening
orchids
music
wine
gambling
good food
chocolate

71

Inventions ~ If Roald Dahl wanted something that didn't exist, he didn't let this stop him—he simply invented it. He created gardening gadgets, made his own hot-air balloons and kites, developed medical cures and devised brain-bending games. His ambition was to invent a silent cigarette lighter—so that he could smoke at night without waking his wife. Luckily for his lungs, he never did. When Theo was hurt in an accident, Roald researched ways to help his son and jointly invented a special valve to drain water from the brain. He and his neighbor also pioneered a type of therapy that helped his first wife to make a full recovery from her strokes. It's still used today by the National Stroke Association.

Random Roald Fact

His favorite famous inventions were the Thermos flask, the penknife, the ballpoint pen, the zipper, cats eye safety reflectors, and razor blades.

jumpsy

jiggyraffes

jumbly

jumpsquiffling

jupping

J is for ...

James and the Giant Peach ~ Did you know that it was nearly called **James and the Giant Cherry**? Eventually, Roald Dahl decided that a peach would be prettier, bigger, and squishier—with a lovely pitted stone in the middle. It was one of the books that Roald was most pleased to have written.

January ~ This was Roald Dahl's least favorite month. He thought the best place to spend an English January was in a hot bath.

"If I had my way I would remove January from the calendar altogether and have an extra July instead."

—ROALD DAHL

Jelly ~ Jelly was Roald Dahl's beautiful black Labrador-cross. Roald often told children that it was really Jelly who wrote the stories and he just took the credit. Jelly is also one of Roald Dahl's dessert inventions. Have you ever wanted to try a dessert that is both crunchy and wibbly-wobbly? You have? Then wait no longer!

Roald's Recipe for Crunchy Jelly

1. Make up some Jell-O following the instructions on the side of the box.
2. Watch the Jell-O as it sets.
3. Are you still watching it?
4. When it is almost ready, mix in a handful of cake decorating sprinkles.
5. When the Jell-O is set, you'll have wibbly-wobbly, Crunchy Jelly!

Jokes ~ Once he'd been told a joke, Roald Dahl never forgot it. He got many of his jokes from his secretary, Wendy. Her children passed them on from the school playground. (See also Knock-knock.)

Jones ~ One of Roald Dahl's boyhood heroes was Jones (nicknamed Joss Spivvis by the Dahl children), the Welsh gardener. Roald would hang out with Joss whenever he could, and in the holidays was by his side all day long. Roald was captivated by Joss's endless stories, and the highlight to the week was their Saturday afternoon trip to Ninian Park to watch Cardiff City football team play. Before the match, they'd stop outside the ground at the whelk stall, where Joss would have jellied eels and Roald would have baked beans and two sausages.

Random Roald Fact
He preferred to write about villains, because
he thought they were more interesting for
the writer and more entertaining for the reader.

K is for ...

kicksy
kidsnatched
kiddles

Kindness ~ Are you a kind person? If you are, Roald Dahl would've been pleased to meet you. If you aren't, he would've wanted to push you down the rubbish chute after Veruca Salt (from **Charlie and the Chocolate Factory**). The BFG was one of his kindest characters, as was the grandmother in **The Witches**. Roald himself was extremely kind, especially with his time. If you lined up to have a book signed, he'd have something special to say to you and everyone else as well, even if he took two or three hours to talk to the whole line.

Kiss ~ Ugh! Although one of Roald Dahl's adult books is called **Kiss Kiss**, he was embarrassed by people kissing in public, and thought you could catch things from it. This poem is from **Rhyme Stew**.

My mother said, "There are no joys
In ever kissing silly boys.
Just one small kiss and one small squeeze
Can land you with some foul disease."

Knock-knock ~ Roald Dahl and his daughter Tessa once compiled
a great collection of knock-knock jokes. Here are just a few. . . .

"Knock-Knock," said the president.

"Who's there?" said the chief spy.

"Courteney."

"Courteney who?"

"Courteney one yet?" said the president.

Knock-Knock!

Who's there?

Sonya.

Sonya who?

Sonya Yetsofar.

Knock-Knock!

Who's there?

Ginger.

Ginger who?

Ginger yourself much when
you fell off the Great Wall of China?

Knock-Knock!

Who's there?

Francis!

Francis who?

Francis full of crazy Frenchmen!

Knowledge ~ Roald Dahl loved learning new things and had a
marvelous memory. Whenever he was interested in something—
photography, sport, cooking, anything!—he had to know
as much about it as possible. One of his favorite
book collections as a child was his mama's set
of battered **Encyclopaedia Britannica**.

Kress, Wendy ~ She worked for Roald Dahl for nearly seven years, transforming his scratchy handwritten pages into neatly typed manuscripts. She also helped answer the many thousands of letters Roald received from his fans.

"It was wonderful to be the very first person to see what he had written."

—WENDY KRESS

Krokaan ~ This mouth-watering Norwegian treat—a crispy kind of toffee made from butter, sugar, and almonds—was one of Roald Dahl's favorites. Krokaan chips in ice cream is out of this world . . . but watch out for your teeth!

"You chewed it and it went crunch and the taste was something you dreamed about for days afterwards."

—ROALD DAHL

lickwishy

lully

langwitch

lolloping

luctuous

L is for...

Languages ~
Roald Dahl's books are read by children all over the world and have been translated into forty-two languages, including Bulgarian, Estonian, Faroese, Friesian, Icelandic, Korean, and Vietnamese. Can you guess which books these are?

Did You Know?
There are estimated to be 6,809 languages in the world.

Leg of lamb ~
Roald Dahl's sense of humor could be very wicked. In one story for adults, a woman murders her husband by

bashing him over the head with a frozen leg of lamb. She then manages to hide the murder weapon from the police while they are searching the house from top to bottom. Can you think how she did it?

WARNING!
Don't try this at home.
It would be very baaaaaad.

Leukemia ~ Roald Dahl died of a form of leukemia (a cancer that affects the blood) on November 23, 1990. He was seventy-four. This is why the Roald Dahl Foundation supports hematology (blood) projects.

Librarians ~ Roald Dahl had a love-hate relationship with librarians. Some liked his books, some didn't. He was puzzled when certain librarians banned **The Witches**, saying that it was anti-women, because the book includes a wonderful, friendly female character—the grandmother. He also created a lovely librarian in **Matilda**, Mrs. Phelps.

Liccy (short for Felicity) ~ Pronounced "Lissy," she is Roald Dahl's second wife. They married in 1983. Among other things, Liccy worked for a fashion magazine and in television and then in an antiques restoration studio. She jointly set up a restoration business in the 1970s called Carvers & Guilders. It did so well, it was granted a Royal Warrant—this meant they could put on their notepaper "By appointment to HM the Queen." After Roald's death, she established the Roald Dahl Foundation, which raises money for charities that were close to the author's heart. (See Family Tree.)

Llandaff ~ Roald Dahl was born in Llandaff, South Wales, in 1916. He met his wife Liccy more than fifty years later and was amazed to discover that she too was born in Llandaff—and on the same street!

Lofty ~ Roald Dahl's fellow Royal Air Force pilots gave him this nickname because he was so tall—just over 6 ½ feet. He also answered to Lampy and Stalky.

Loneliness ~ James is Roald Dahl's loneliest character. So lonely, in fact, that he has only insects for company. They turn out to be the greatest friends of all, however. Roald knew what it was like to be lonely when he was an airman during the war. He also spent many lonely hours in the Hut. As soon as he finished work for the day, he strolled up to

Gipsy House, where he was guaranteed to be surrounded by family and friends. Writing must be one of the loneliest careers of all.

Louis ~ Roald Dahl's older half-brother was his mentor. Louis often took Roald for a spin on the back of his motorbike and taught him all about fishing. Roald might have caught the inventing bug from him—Louis invented a wonderful boomerang-like toy called—guess what?—a Skilly Wonka. (See Family Tree.)

Lucky ~ When he was first flying in Africa, Roald Dahl wrote to his mother, telling her how lucky he felt to be whizzing and soaring through the skies. He really *was* lucky. Most of the pilots he trained with didn't survive the war, and Roald nearly didn't when his plane crashed in the Libyan desert and burst into flames. He managed to drag himself out before the whole thing blew up.

Lucy ~ Roald's youngest daughter (nicknamed Lukey by Roald) was born in 1965 and became a keen horse rider. At gymkhanas she would always look out for a yellow bobble hat in the crowd—Roald would wear it to let her know that he was there. (See Family Tree.)

murderful

moocheling

muckfrumping

maggotwise

micies

mispise

muggled

M is for ...

The Magic Finger ~ This story was originally called **The Almost Ducks**. The characters were to be Mr. and Mrs. Almost, and their unlucky children were to be magically transformed into ducks. Instead, it's the Gregg family who are at the receiving end of the magic finger, which has the power to ... Well, that would be telling, wouldn't it?

Mama ~ This is what Roald Dahl called his mother—Sofie Magdalene Hesselberg Dahl. She was an incredible woman and the most important

influence in Roald's life. She was widowed when he was only three years old and she was pregnant with her fifth child. From then on, she brought up her children single-handed, taking them to Tenby in Pembrokeshire every Easter and Norway every summer. She inspired one of the loveliest characters in **The Witches**—the grandmother. Sofie was a wonderful storyteller and had an amazing memory for detail. (See Family Tree.)

Master forger ~ Roald Dahl once painted a copy of a Cézanne landscape and hung it on his sitting-room wall. It fools everyone but the real art experts.

Matilda ~ This book might have been very different. In Roald Dahl's original draft, the main character was a boy called Jimmy. Then he became Matilda, who was a wicked girl who died from exhaustion when she used her powers to lift a truck off a minibus. Like his readers, Roald was delighted with the final version of **Matilda**, which had been an idea for twenty years before it became a finished book.

Maze ~ There's an amazing maze in the garden of Roald Dahl's home, with surprises at every turn. Some of the best lines from his books—chosen by family, friends, and those who worked with him—are carved into slabs of York stone dotted throughout the maze. Here are a couple of quotations in the maze:

Mary, Mary quite contrary
How does your garden grow?
"I live with a brat in a high-rise flat,
So how in the world would I know?"

"I know full well my tummy's bulging
But oh how I adore indulging."

Meanest man alive ~
Roald Dahl always used to say that the meanest man alive was the kind of person who would buy a turkey at Christmas, cut it in two, and freeze half for Easter.

Meccano ~
When Roald Dahl was given a Meccano set one Christmas, he immediately put his thinking cap on. He soon had the bright idea of making a machine that would drop a waterfall onto

passersby. He built this mischievous machine with great care and it worked splendidly— but unfortunately, his two lady victims were not amused. Result? The Meccano set was confiscated for the rest of the holiday.

The Minpins ~ Although he loved Quentin Blake's work, Roald Dahl realized that this picture book needed a totally different style of illustration. A competition was held among several illustrators and it was Patrick Benson's work that Roald liked most. His beautifully detailed pictures suit the story perfectly.

Missing! ~ Roald Dahl ruthlessly chopped two revolting children out of the final version of **Charlie and the Chocolate Factory**. Marvin Prune was a conceited boy, while Miranda Mary Piker was allowed to do anything she wanted. (Apart from appear in one of Roald's books, it would seem.)

Mole alert! ~ Roald Dahl didn't attack the moles that dared to create molehills all over his garden. He deafened them instead. Here's how he did it:

1. First, he buried an empty wine bottle near a molehill, leaving the neck sticking out.

2. When the wind blew across the bottle, it made a humming sound that went on…

3. …and on…

4. …and on…

5. …until the noise drove the moles so crazy that they moved out of Roald's garden! Luckily there were no neighbors around Gipsy House.

Mozart ~ Dahl was fascinated to learn that the eighteenth-century classical composer Wolfgang Amadeus Mozart was already composing music when he was only five years old. This was one of the things that made him realize that adults often underestimate children. So he created the brilliant Matilda, who taught herself to read when she was just three years old.

Mushrooming ~ Mushroom-picking was one of Roald Dahl's hobbies in later life. He loved to go out early in the morning, in his gumboots and with his dog Chopper for company, to gather mushrooms, hidden like jewels among the cowpats in the local field. (Hope he didn't get them mixed up.)

Did You Know?
In France, you can take your mushrooms to the pharmacist to make sure they're not poisonous. (Do not try this yourself!)

Liccy Dahl's Recipe for Mushrooms on Toast

1. Fry VERY fresh mushrooms with lots of butter.
2. Pop them on to a hot piece of toast.
3. Drizzle the juices on top of the mushrooms and toast and sprinkle them with a little salt.
4. Eat at once.
5. Mmm . . .

Music ~ Roald Dahl liked listening to music by Beethoven in the morning—he hoped some of the great composer's genius would rub off on him before he started work.

Did You Know?
Beethoven composed some of his best work when he was deaf.

Mystery motorcyclist ~ As a daredevil seventeen-year-old, Roald Dahl bought an old motorbike (a 500cc Ariel) and drove it to Repton School for his last term. He kept it a few miles away from the school and—disguised in a huge scarf and goggles—roared around the lanes whenever he could get out. Not a single teacher or prefect recognized him. He once said, "It gave me an amazing feeling of winged majesty and of independence."

N is for ...

Neal, Patricia ~ The Hollywood actress became Roald Dahl's first wife in Trinity Church in New York in July 1953. It was such a hot day that Roald ripped out the lining of his suit to make it cooler. Patricia won an Academy Award—an Oscar—for her role in the film **Hud** (1963), in which she starred with Paul Newman. She and Roald were married for thirty years, had five children together, and divorced in 1983. (See Family Tree.)

Newspaper and string ~ Roald Dahl was a great present-giver, always finding just the right gift for the right person. He wrapped his marvelous presents in newspaper and tied them with string. He also sometimes "gift-wrapped" presents in flowerpots!

New York City ~ Roald Dahl lived in New York after the Second World War. He spent his time working on short stories for adults, trying hard to become established as a writer. It was a place he came to hate when his four-month-old son was hit in his stroller by a taxi.

Nitpicking ~ Roald Dahl enjoyed research and made sure that his facts were spot on. Howiver, he woz a tirrible speller.

Norway ~ Both Roald Dahl's parents were from Norway. They spoke Norwegian to each other, and Roald and his sisters learned Norwegian before English. Roald visited Norway many times and took his own family there for holidays. They spent their time boating, fishing, snorkeling, and visiting a never-ending stream of Norwegian relatives. Do you know what this says? **Jeg er en Roald Dahl vifte**.

Nose ~ Dahl's nose had a rough life. It was nearly chopped off in an accident during his very first car journey. Then it was bashed in when his plane crash-landed during the Second World War. After the crash, the surgeon rebuilt his nose in the style of the terribly dashing silent-film star Rudolf Valentino. Ask a really old person—they might remember who he was.

Answer: I am a Roald Dahl fan.

"The ear, nose, and throat man pulled my nose out of the back of my head, and shaped it, and now it looks just as before except that it's a little bent about."

—ROALD DAHL

Nurses ~ Roald Dahl thought nurses were wonderful, and made up lovely nicknames for all the ones who helped him on his many stays in hospital.

O is for... *offenly*

official photographer ~
Roald Dahl took the official photos on an expedition to Newfoundland when he was young. Look out for these splendid black-and-white photos at the Roald Dahl Museum and Story Centre! He also took some good photographs when he was in Africa.

Oil ~
When Roald Dahl finished school in 1934 he turned down his mother's suggestion that he should go to the university because he desperately wanted to see the world.

His first job was with the Shell Oil Company. After training in London and then selling oil in Somerset to old ladies, he was sent to work in the mysterious and exotic country of Tanganyika (now part of Tanzania) in East Africa—a dream come true.

Olivanas ~ This was a treat that Roald Dahl learned from his mother and used to make for his own children. You can enjoy it, too. Just mash up a banana with a few drops of olive oil. For some reason, the olive oil heightens the flavor of the banana and turns it into a delicious syrupy paste. If you're feeling very wicked, finish off your Olivana with a dollop of whipped cream. Yum-yum!

Olivia ~ Born in 1955, Roald Dahl's first child, Olivia, was very imaginative. She said that she carried an invisible imp on each shoulder—one good and one bad. Tragically, she caught measles and died when she was just seven years old—there was no vaccination program at the time. She was buried in Little Missenden and Roald never got over her death. He created an alpine garden on her grave that contained about 120 plant species, and he visited it regularly. (See Family Tree.)

Onions ~ These were Roald Dahl's favorite vegetable. He liked to grow giant onions because he enjoyed their special mild-sweet taste, especially when they were raw. The biggest onions he ever grew were a variety called Robinson's Mammoth Improved Onion, which weighed an average of 3 pounds each! These monsters were perfect for making onion rings and onion soup. Sometimes there is an onion left on Roald's grave.

Ooh la la! ~ Two of the best things about France, according to Roald Dahl, were the food and the wine. His favorite French dishes were foie gras (a very rich goose liver pâté), mussels, and snails!

Random Roald Fact

His soup had to be piping hot.
He hated cold or lukewarm soup
and would noisily complain
about it to waiters, much to the
embarrassment of his children.

Ooops! ~ Roald Dahl enjoyed cleaning up old paintings in his shed. This involved gently brushing the surface of the painting to remove the dirt, but once he accidentally cleaned off the painting as well as the dirt. Let's hope it wasn't a valuable work of art!

Openings ~ Roald Dahl made sure readers were entranced by his stories from the very first page. Can you guess which books these first sentences belong to?

1. What a lot of hairy-faced men there are around nowadays.
2. Not far from where I live there is a queer old empty wooden house standing all by itself on the side of the road.
3. In fairy tales, witches always wear silly black hats and black cloaks, and they ride on broomsticks.
4. Until he was four, James Henry Trotter had a happy life.

"Grab them by the throat with the first sentence."
—ROALD DAHL

1. The Twits   2. The Giraffe and the Pelly and Me   3. The Witches   4. James and the Giant Peach

Operations ~ Roald Dahl had a great respect for doctors and went under the surgeon's knife many times for operations on his adenoids, his nose, his hips, and his back.

Ophelia ~ Roald Dahl's daughter Ophelia was born in 1964 and was soon nicknamed Don Mini by her brother. Just like Danny in **Danny the Champion of the World**, she learned to drive when she was very young. Roald taught her in the orchard of Gipsy House when she was only ten years old. A few months later, the mischievous Ophelia borrowed the car, drove to the local village, and then broke down. When she phoned her father to be rescued, he was more annoyed that she'd interrupted his writing than by her underage driving. (See Family Tree.)

Orchids ~ Roald Dahl was an orchid expert and even won a gold medal from the Royal Horticultural Society. He enjoyed pottering around his orchid house in the garden at Gipsy House, which is now the snooker room. He loved orchids for their perfection.

Ordinary ~ Roald Dahl always said it was a terrible mistake to meet writers you admired, for in the flesh they were bound to be very ordinary. He told his young fans that he was ordinary and said it was much better to imagine a rather unusual, romantic figure with a red beard, dressed perhaps in a flowing green cloak—with magic in his fingers. Roald was never ordinary.

Orphanage ~ The building that inspired the orphanage in **The BFG** still stands in the High Street in Great Missenden. It is now the site of the Roald Dahl Museum and Story Centre.

Random Roald Fact

The young Roald Dahl started speaking late, at about three years old, and his first words, in Norwegian, were "Papa's slippers are under the bed."

puddlenuts
pifflefizz
prunty
phizz-whizzing
pigwinkle

P is for ...

Papa ~ Roald Dahl never really knew his father since, tragically, he died of pneumonia in 1920, when Roald was only three. Harald Dahl came from a small town near Oslo in Norway and, from humble beginnings, he built up a prosperous shipbroking business (shipbrokers refuel and supply ships when they come into port). It was often said that Harald died of a broken heart after the death of his daughter Astri two months before. Roald always missed his father and tried to be the sort of parent his children would like and trust. He knew that the best parents were sparky, just like the father in **Danny the Champion of the World**. (See Family Tree.)

Pea soup ~ At Roald Dahl's boarding school, older pupils were allowed to cook for themselves. Here's Roald's recipe for how NOT to cook pea soup:

1. Place can of soup in front of the fire to heat.
2. Leave there for far too long, preferably until the can is bulging.

3. Hold an umbrella in front of you while piercing the can.

4. Stand well back and watch boiling-hot soup spurt out of the can and all over the room.

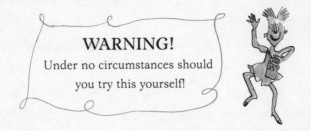

WARNING!
Under no circumstances should
you try this yourself!

Peach tree ~ A peach tree that Roald Dahl planted in his garden at Gipsy House didn't produce a single peach until the film of **James and the Giant Peach** was premiered in London. Then it grew just one perfect peach and died the following year.

The Perfect Murder ~ Roald Dahl's idea for the perfect murder was to bury an oyster in the garden until it went bad and then serve it with eleven others to the intended victim. Terrible food poisoning would follow and result in death—a death that would simply be put down to one bad shellfish. Never to be tried in real life!

Pesto ~ In 2003, a new dog moved into Gipsy House—a tiny Jack Russell puppy called Pesto. He is Chopper's great-great-great-great-great grandson. Roald Dahl would have loved him.

Photographers ~ Roald Dahl hated having his picture taken but loved taking photos himself.

Piggy ~ This was the affectionate nickname given to Roald Dahl's cook in the house he shared with some other men who worked for Shell in Africa. Piggy's best recipe was baked potatoes stuffed with crabmeat. Roald and his friends found it so delicious they ate it for supper twice a week.

Poaching ~ Roald Dahl's local butcher had a passion for poaching and told Roald how to hunt animals that lived on other people's land. Roald found the idea thrilling but never caught a pheasant himself, unlike Danny and his father in **Danny the Champion of the World**. And his incredibly illegal research led to a best-selling children's book.

> Bad: Poaching animals in the woods in the dead of night.
> Good: Poaching eggs in hot water.

Potions ~

Roald Dahl mixed marvelous bedtime drinks for his children and called them "witches' potions." They contained ingredients such as canned peaches blended with milk and pink, blue, or green food coloring. Maybe this is where the idea came from for George's wicked potions.

Presidents and prime ministers ~

Just as Willy Wonka and Charlie and his family met the president of the United States in **Charlie and the Great Glass Elevator**, so too did Roald Dahl. He was invited to dinner at the White House because the president's wife, Eleanor Roosevelt, liked his **Gremlins** story and read it to her grandchildren. Roald was shaking with excitement on his first visit, but he had such a good time that he was invited back. He got to know Franklin Roosevelt better when he stayed at the president's country house, Hyde Park. Roald also played poker with Harry Truman (who later became the U.S. president) and met British prime minister, Margaret Thatcher, to whom he gave a copy of **Going Solo**.

Private ~ No one was allowed to look at Roald Dahl's diary. At school he kept it in his lunchbox, which was always locked. At home he hid it inside a cookie tin, which was inside a toiletries bag, which was hung from the highest branch of a huge chestnut tree at the bottom of the garden. He climbed the tree every day—unless it was pouring with rain—to write in privacy. On wet days, he kept his thoughts to himself.

> **Random Roald Fact**
> He didn't like going to the cinema or theater. Because he was so tall, he found the seats incredibly uncomfortable.

Q is for . . .

quicksy

quogwinkles

quicky

Questions ~ Roald Dahl's readers were often so excited when they met him that they were far too nervous to speak, never mind ask a question. His wife would start them off by asking Roald something like, "How many grapefruit did you eat for breakfast this morning?" One question that left him speechless was, "What happened to Thwaites (his friend with ratitis in **Boy**)?"

Quiz ~ So, how much do YOU know about Roald Dahl? Are you a REAL fan? Put your thinking cap on and see how many of this A–Z of quiz questions you can answer. The answer to Question A begins with an A, the answer to Question B begins with a B—and so on. But beware! You might find some of the answers in this book, but you won't find all of them here. You might have to delve into Roald Dahl's actual books to complete the quiz. . . .

A. Which bits of Roald were removed by a doctor when he was eight years old?

B. What color is a witch's spit?

C. What gushed over Willy Wonka's waterfall?

D. What did Roald once hide in a jar of sweets?

E. Roald once wrote a rather slow-moving love story. Can you guess the title?

F. What is the name of the pale-green fizzy drink that fills the BFG and Sophie with bubbles?

G. Who does George feed his Marvellous Medicine to?

H. What was the Dahl family's boat called?

I. What did Roald keep in two battered exercise books?

J. Who lived happily ever after in a "stone" house in New York City?

K. What was the name of Roald's favorite toffee-like Norwegian treat?

L. Which of Roald's daughters was bullied on the way to school?

M. Which tiny creatures lived in the Forest of Sin?

N. What part of his body did Roald almost lose in a car accident?

O. Who works in Willy Wonka's factory?

P. What did Roald eat for lunch every day?

Q. The BFG blows a dream into the bedroom of a very famous person. Who?

R. Which little fairy-tale character was this?

> The small girl smiles. One eyelid flickers.
>
> She whips a pistol from her knickers.

S. Which aunts were ironed flat by the giant peach?

T. What did Roald often warm for a prefect at Repton?

U. When he worked in London, Roald always made sure that he carried one particular thing with him. What was it?

V. Which are the scariest and most dangerous aliens in the universe (according to Willy Wonka)?

W. What does Mrs. Twit mix into her husband's spaghetti?

X. What did doctors use to photograph Roald's insides? (Well, you try to think of another answer that begins with X!)

Y. What was Roald's favorite color?

Z. Which invention did Roald really admire? (Clue: it was better than buttons.)

Adenoids—Blue—Chocolate—Dead mouse—Esio Trot—Frobscottle—
Grandma—Hard Black Stinker—Ideas—James Henry Trotter—Krokaan—
Lucy—Minpins—Nose—Oompa-Loompas—Prawns—The Queen—
Red Riding Hood—Sponge and Spiker—Toilet seat—Umbrella—
Vermicious Knids—Worms—X-rays—Yellow—Zipper

R is for . . .

Raspberries ~ Roald Dahl grew these luscious fruits when he was very young. He loved them, in a dribbly, sticky way. In Norway, his aunts used to sit with a big bowl of yellow "mutter" raspberries and a needle to hook out the maggots lurking inside.

Readathon® ~ Since 1984, Readathon® has raised millions of pounds for children's charities in the UK. Roald Dahl thought the sponsored reading event, created by Brough Girling, was a fantastic idea and became the Readathon® patron in 1988. Not only do children get to read their favorite books, but they get paid for doing it and this money helps others—all at the same time!

Reading ~ Roald Dahl thought that reading was ESSENTIAL! Without it, you can't do anything in life. He didn't judge people on what they liked to read, as long as they read something.

Real people ~ Roald Dahl often based his characters on people he knew but concealed their identity by making up new names—his inspiration for this was the telephone directory.

Red-Hot Smoke-Belching Gruncher ~ This is the name of the terrible beast from **The Minpins**. It's very, very scary.

Revolting Rhymes ~ They're repulsive, they're rude, and they're really really revolting. They're also highly recommended. If you haven't read them, buy a copy without delay! Roald Dahl made these up in the bath and that's a good place to read them.

Rhyme Stew ~ Roald Dahl loved tinkering with fairy tales and nursery rhymes when he was between books, waiting for the next big idea to come along. **Rhyme Stew** was the result, and although this collection of rhymes was written for adults, many older children dip into it, too. It's full

of snappy rhymes to get your teeth into—and some even bite back! This snippet is from "The Dentist and the Crocodile."

He opened wide his massive jaws.
It was a fearsome sight—
At least three hundred pointed teeth,
all sharp and shining white.
The dentist kept himself well clear.
He stood two yards away.
He chose the longest probe he had
to search out the decay.

The Roald Dahl Children's Gallery ~ This is part of
the Buckinghamshire County Museum. You can go inside James's giant peach to see the insect collection or ride in Willy Wonka's Great Glass Elevator to find out about space flight. You can travel by television like Mike Teavee in **Charlie and the Chocolate Factory**, too, and discover how your TV works. This totally brilliant interactive museum is the only one of its kind in the world! Check out the website at www.buckscc.gov.uk/museum/dahl

Roald Dahl Club ~ Did you know you could join the Roald
Dahl Club? You do now. Log on to www.roalddahl.com right away!

THE ROALD DAHL FOUNDATION

Doing **wonkalicious** things

Providing practical support for children with
brain, blood, and literacy problems

What is the Roald Dahl Foundation?

As well as being a great storyteller, Roald Dahl was also a man who
gave generously of his time and money to help people in need,
especially children. After he died in 1990, his widow, Felicity, set up
the Roald Dahl Foundation to continue this generous tradition.
Its support spreads far and wide. Since it began, the Foundation
has given over £4 million across the UK.

The Foundation aims to help children and young
people in practical ways and in three areas that
were particularly important to Roald during his
lifetime: neurology, hematology, and literacy. It
makes grants to hospitals and charities, as well
as to individual children and their families.

Supporting the Roald Dahl Foundation

Funded partly through its original endowment, the Foundation also benefits from a range of fund-raising, most notably the national sponsored reading event Readathon®. In addition, it is proud of the Friends of the Roald Dahl Foundation, who arrange a program of local events, the many schoolchildren who fund-raise on its behalf, and the Payroll Giving supporters. Finally, it is able to benefit from an ambitious program of new orchestral music for children based on Roald's stories and rhymes, specially commissioned on its behalf.

To find out more about the
Roald Dahl Foundation,
visit the Web site at
www.roalddahlfoundation.org

The Roald Dahl Foundation
is a registered charity no. 1004230

"Tremendous Things Are in Store for You!"

Are you one of Roald Dahl's biggest fans? If you are, then we have got some splendiferous news for you!

As you probably know, Roald lived in Great Missenden, a quiet village in Buckinghamshire where he wrote all of his stories for kids. But did you know that Great Missenden is the most scrumdiddlyumptious place in the world? This is where you'll find the Roald Dahl Museum and Story Centre.

The Museum and Story Centre tells the eventful tale of Roald's life, using photographs and film. Interactive displays help you to discover more about his Norwegian family, his school days, his time as a Second World War pilot, and how he became a world-famous writer. It is also jam-packed with stuff about how to write, a replica of Roald's writing hut, and facts about other brilliant authors. You will even get the chance to make up stories of your

own! At the heart of the Museum and Story Centre is an amazing archive full of things that have never been seen before, including the original handwritten drafts of many of Roald's books, corrected typescripts, fifty years of letters, and a lifetime of family photographs.

For more information on the Roald Dahl Museum and Story Centre, visit www.roalddahlmuseum.org

GREAT MISSENDEN · ROALD DAHL · THE HOME OF ·

The Roald Dahl Museum and Story Centre is a registered charity no. 1085853

Roald Dahl's Revolting Recipes and Roald Dahl's Even More Revolting Recipes ~

Stuffed with scrumdiddlyumptious instructions, these books show the hungry reader how to prepare recipes such as Liquid Chocolate Mixed by Waterfall (from **Charlie and the Chocolate Factory**) and Mosquitoes' Toes and Wampfish Roes Most Delicately Fried (from **James and the Giant Peach**). Er, mmm . . . urgh!

Royal Air Force ~

Roald Dahl joined the Royal Air Force in Nairobi, Kenya, in 1939, just after Britain declared war on Germany. He went on his first solo flight after just seven hours and forty minutes of training and went into combat territory with only eight months' training in all. War brought Roald many hardships and injuries but gave him moments of great happiness, too—for example, flying in his Tiger Moth over the Kenyan Highlands. Later, he flew a Hurricane on many missions and took part in the Battle of Athens in April 1941. You can read all about this in **Going Solo**.

My Hurricane, Haifa

S is for ...

Sandals ~ When Quentin Blake started his drawings for **The BFG**, he showed the giant wearing boots, but that didn't feel quite right. So, Roald Dahl sent him one of his own old Norwegian sandals—and they were perfect.

Satisfaction ~ Roald Dahl was never satisfied with what he wrote, with the exception of **Matilda**.

> **"Writing is mainly perspiration, not inspiration."**
>
> —ROALD DAHL

Sausages ~ If you were invited to supper at Roald Dahl's house, he would probably cook you sausages. Then he would tell you that only he and the queen had those particular sausages.

School ~ Roald Dahl was so famous he had a school named after him in the Netherlands. Liccy still receives letters from the Roald Dahl Basics School—and she wears the T-shirt.

School reports ~ Here is one of Roald Dahl's school reports. In another, his English teacher described Roald as being "quite incapable of marshalling his thoughts on paper." From these you would never have guessed he'd go on to be a great writer.

REPTON SCHOOL TERMINAL REPORT.

Term ending *July 26* 1932

Form *Rª* Boy's Name *R Dahl* Age: *15* yrs. *5* mo. } at beginning of Term.

Place for Term in all subjects combined. *12* Number in Form *12* Average Age of Form: *16* yrs. *9* mo. }

" " First Half Term *12*
" " Second " " *12*

REMARKS.

English Subjects.
Hist. 6. Has done better this term: his work has sometimes been really good.
Engl. Satisfactory work: ideas limited. RCB
Scrip. Consistently idle: too pleased with himself. HJS.

Classics — Latin or German. Set III
Satisfactory progress for me. M.HO.

French. 12. During the 2nd half term he has produced better results. I have little doubt that he often tries to hide idleness behind a vail of stupidity. His regrowth may perhaps excuse some of his apathy. SJ

Drawing.

House and General Behaviour. He is so large that it is often difficult to remember how young he is. It is true however that he put more effort into his work; he is capable of doing quite respectable work.

At the best he could produce by gods way.

B.S. 46.

Secret diaries ~ Roald Dahl

believed that there were two kinds of
diaries—the secret-thoughts diary and
the what-happened-to-me-today diary.
His advice to would-be diary-writers was
that before writing a single word, it was
absolutely essential to find a top-secret hiding place. (He knew that even
the nicest mothers would be quite unable to resist reading a diary if they
found it.) Roald never revealed what happened to his own diaries. Did he
burn them or bury them? (See also Hiding places.)

Secrets ~ Roald Dahl just couldn't keep them! An example of this

was the surprise that he thought up for his wife, Liccy—to buy a puppy.
The plan was to fetch the puppy, put him in a basket, and leave it on her
bed. But the secret was too hard to keep and he "let the dog out of the
basket" and ended up taking Liccy to choose him herself. Who was the
puppy? None other than the famous Chopper.

Serious science ~ Roald Dahl loved to put his curious mind

to the test by inventing new devices designed to solve the trickiest of
problems. When his son was seriously ill, he helped to develop a valve
that drained liquid from the brain. Although Theo Dahl recovered
without needing the valve, it was used to treat over 2,000 children.

$\int$having ~

Roald Dahl didn't like shaving. To make it more fun, he would pretend that he was playing golf and, just as he tried to get from the tee to the hole in only three shots, he tried to shave his chin in three strokes of his razor blade. The alternative to shaving—a big hairy beard—was far worse, according to Roald.

$\int$hhhh! ~

During the Easter holidays in Roald Dahl's childhood, his family always took a boat trip to Caldy Island. Roald was astonished by the monks in the island's monastery. He knew they had all taken a vow of silence, but he couldn't imagine ever being able to stay quiet himself. Could you?

$\int$hiny $\int$tone ~

When he visited Australia, Roald Dahl chatted with children in Mintabe, where precious stones called opals are found. He asked one of the boys if he ever found opals and, later, the boy did find a beautiful piece of rock with veins of opal running through it. He sent it to Roald, who kept it on his treasure table. The rock is now set in the path that leads to Roald's writing hut, glistening and glowing green and blue.

Shrinks! ~ Just like Mrs. Twit, as Roald Dahl grew older he got the dreaded shrinks and lost about 3 inches from his 6 1/2-foot height. This was because of all the laminectomy operations he had after his plane crash, when bits were removed from his spine.

Silver ball ~ About the size of a tennis ball and weighing 10 1/2 ounces, is the silver ball that Roald Dahl molded from the silver papers of his daily chocolate bar wrappers when he worked in London.

Silver Pencil Award ~ Roald Dahl won the Dutch Silver Pencil Award so many times that, in the end, he told the judges they must give it to someone else. And who did they choose to present the award to the next winner? Roald, of course.

Silver screen ~ Many of Roald Dahl's books—including **Charlie and the Chocolate Factory**, **Matilda**, **Danny the Champion of the World**, and **James and the Giant Peach**—made the successful leap from the page to the silver screen of cinema. More films are on the way.

snozzling

slimewanglers

scuddle

Random Roald Fact

He loved oxtail stew.

---

squinky

scrumplet

scotch-hopper

Skilly Wonka ~ When the film of **Charlie and the Chocolate Factory** was released in 1971, Roald Dahl received a letter from a Mr. Bill Wonka who lived in Blue Hill, Nebraska, complaining that the author had stolen and used his name. Roald promptly replied that he'd actually gotten the name from a boomerang-like toy, invented by his half-brother Louis, which they called a Skilly Wonka.

Small print ~ Roald Dahl was concerned about every single part of his books—from the words and the illustrations to the cover and even the size of the text. He hated it when words were printed so small that they were difficult to read.

Smarties ~ Roald Dahl adored Smarties chocolate candy, and so did his dog. Chopper received eight a day—four after lunch and four after supper. (Chocolate can be harmful to some dogs. Never give a dog chocolate without its owner's permission.)

Smile, please! ~ Photography was one of Roald Dahl's hobbies. While at school, he made himself extra pocket money by taking passport photos for his fellow pupils. He won two prizes for his photographs.

Snailbox Lady ~

Aha! Surely this must be a seriously slow pet? A sluggish sloth or a tired tiger? Er, no . . . not quite. This is what Roald Dahl named his very first greyhound—a rocket of a racing dog. An evening out at the White City Stadium in London, watching Snailbox Lady whizz round the track, was Roald's idea of heaven.

Snakes, scorpions, and mosquitoes ~

While living in East Africa in the 1930s, Roald Dahl had to put up with these tropical terrors and many more besides. You can find out about it all in **Going Solo**.

Snooker ~

Roald Dahl loved snooker so much that he had his very own table at home. He played regularly with friends from the village, including the local builder Wally Saunders. The only female player was Roald's daughter Ophelia.

Sometime Never ~ Roald Dahl's first adult novel was published in 1948. It was a fantasy about gremlins, the Second World War, and the end of the world. He never liked it and wasn't sorry when it went out of print.

Sophie ~ The BFG's best friend is named after a real Sophie, Roald Dahl's granddaughter, although in the earliest version of the story the main character was a little boy called Jody! She is the only family member whose name was used for a human character in one of his books. Sophie Dahl is now a supermodel—and a writer. (See Family Tree.)

Spelling ~ You might be surprised to learn that Roald Dahl was a terrible speller. However, he loved playing around with words and inventing new ones. **The BFG** is overflowing with frogsquinkers, buzzwangles, frobscottle, and lots more whoppsy-good words.

> ### Random Roald Fact
> Spiders—he adored them.

Sporty ~ Roald Dahl was a natural sportsman and loved all kinds of sports—hockey, soccer, squash, and cricket to name a few. He was a very good boxer, perhaps because of his lo-o-o-ong arms.

Stalky ~ This was the nickname given to Roald Dahl by the one and only Walt Disney when they briefly worked together in Hollywood. This was because Walt couldn't pronounce Roald's name and also due to the fact that Roald was tall and gangly like a giant beanstalk.

Stars and Stripes ~ No, not the American flag. At Roald Dahl's boarding school in Weston-super-Mare, stars were given for good work. The teachers were so mean that they usually gave quarter stars—four had to be collected to make a star. Stripes were given for poor work or bad behavior.

Stepdaughters ~ Roald Dahl was very fond of Liccy's daughters, Neisha, Charlotte, and Lorina, and they became good friends with Roald's children from his first marriage.

Sticky head ~ During an adventure holiday to Newfoundland when he was seventeen, mosquitoes annoyed Roald Dahl so much that he shaved his head and covered it in tar to stop them from biting him.

HELPFUL NON-STICKY ADVICE

Pharmacists now sell insect repellents that
don't involve bald heads or gloopy stuff.

Sunshine ~ One treasure kept in Roald Dahl's writing hut was a music box that needed neither clockwork nor batteries. It played a tune as soon as the sun shone on it.

Sweets ~ Roald Dahl's glove compartment in his car was always full of sweets. When he picked up his two eldest daughters and their friends from school, sweets were given out to the person who told the best story on the journey home.

T is for ...

Taboo ~ Roald Dahl risked the anger of critics with his fearless approach to writing. He was probably the first person to mention farting in a children's book. He also wanted his readers to do daring things and encouraged parents not to be overprotective—Roald thoroughly approved of children walking on walls and climbing trees.

Taxi drivers ~ Roald Dahl liked the idea of London taxi drivers "doing the knowledge"—learning about every single street in London before they could get a taxi licence. And taxi drivers liked him. They argued about who was to pick Roald up at Gipsy House, because he was always such an entertaining passenger. Roald's own sense of direction was rubbish!

Teacher, favorite ~ Just like Miss Honey in **Matilda**, Mrs. O'Connor was a brilliant teacher. She ran an English class at Roald Dahl's school every Saturday morning, and her visit was the highlight of his week. Roald had always liked stories, but she gave him a real love of literature, and by the time he was thirteen, he was an insatiable reader and a good writer. Without Mrs. O'Connor, Charlie and Willy Wonka and James and Mr. Twit and the Grand High Witch and the BFG might never have been invented. Can you imagine anything worse? No, nor can we.

Teacher, red-faced ~
Roald Dahl was sent heaps of letters from schools, and in his replies he often chose to embarrass the teachers. His letters were always very friendly, beginning with something like: "Hello, Class Three and your gorgeous teacher Mrs. Smiley." Then there was a poem. This one was sent to classes around the world:

> Dear children far across the sea,
> How nice of you to write to me.
> I love to hear the things you say
> When you are miles and miles away.
> All children, and I think I'm right,
> Are nicer when they're out of sight!

Tessa ~
Roald Dahl's second daughter was born in 1957. She was originally named Chantal ... until Pat and Roald spotted the rhyme (Chantal Dahl) and renamed her Tessa. Tessa has followed in her father's

footsteps and written books for both children and adults. She inherited Roald's wicked sense of humor, too. (See Family Tree.)

Theo ~ Roald Dahl's only son was born in 1960. He ran an antique shop with Roald called Dahl & Son. Just like his father, he loves golf and snooker. (See Family Tree.)

Thwack! ~ It was long and it was yellow and it curved round at the end like a walking stick. Throughout his school days, it was the one thing that Roald Dahl detested more than anything else—the cane. The most talented thwackers could place each stinging stroke directly on top of the one before, leaving a perfect single bruise across the bottom. Roald never agreed with the use of the cane, not even when he was older. He thought its use should be banned in schools. Now it is.

> **"It wasn't simply an instrument for beating you. It was a weapon for wounding."**
>
> —ROALD DAHL

Time ~ Roald Dahl didn't like to waste a single minute. Once, when a hospital appointment was postponed, he threw a coat over his pajamas and spent the time visiting a nearby school instead.

Titles ~ Roald Dahl always left the title of his book till last—when the whole story had been written.

Toilet paper ~ Roald Dahl's books are sold all over the world and appear in many different languages. The first Chinese edition was printed on paper so thin it looked like toilet paper.

Toilet-seat warmer extraordinaire ~ At Repton School, the younger pupils acted as servants for the older boys. This often meant tidying their study or running errands. But Roald Dahl was given a really odd job to do. He sat on the toilet in a chilly outhouse, making sure that the seat was warm and toasty enough for the house prefect's bottom!

P.S. Roald would never have used the word toilet. He preferred to say lavatory or WC.

Did You Know?

The most expensive bathroom in the world is in Hong Kong and it cost $4.3 million! It is made of 24-carat gold. The ceiling is decorated with rubies, sapphires, and emeralds.

Treasure table ~ This was the table in the Hut on which
Roald Dahl kept his collection of special things.

silver
wrapper ball

spine shavings

Hurricane
model
plane

rock
containing
opal

electric
pencil
sharpener

Roald's
femur

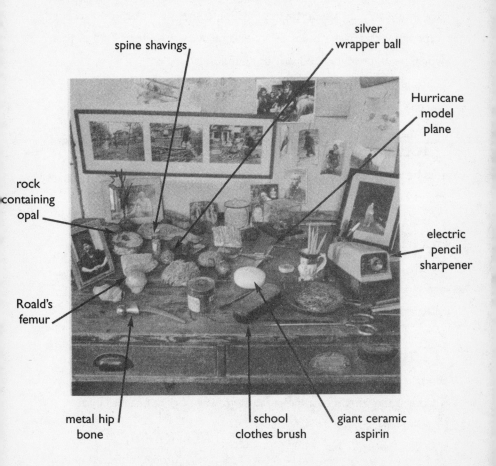

metal hip
bone

school
clothes brush

giant ceramic
aspirin

Treats ~ Treats were an essential part of Roald Dahl's life. A treat could be a first new potato, broad bean, or lettuce from the garden, or a field mushroom or a superb chestnut. Sometimes he would even surprise someone with a plane ticket or a weekend away. A different kind of treat would be an unannounced visit to a school, causing chaos for the teachers and a great deal of fun for the children.

Trolls ~ Roald Dahl's mother told her children—and later her grandchildren—stories from Norway of trolls, witches, and strange mythical creatures that lived in dark pine forests. Does this remind you of a grandmotherly figure from any of Roald's books?

Trotter ~ A pig's foot. Or a horse that trots. Or . . . there was something else, I'm sure. Oh, yes! Trotter is the surname of the greatest grower of giant peaches in children's literature.

Trunchbull, Miss ~ Can you think of a nastier character than Miss Trunchbull? (No, we didn't think so.)

Tuck box ~ At Roald Dahl's boarding school, no pupil would be without their tuck box. This was a small wooden trunk (with a strong padlock) packed full of cake, biscuits, oranges, strawberry jam, chocolate, and other treats. One of Roald's friends even kept a pet frog in his, which he fed slugs.

TV ~ Roald Dahl thought that too much television was bad. He felt that children would be far better occupied reading books. See what happens to TV-mad Mike Teavee in **Charlie and the Chocolate Factory**.

Twitchy ~ Roald Dahl was once described as being "twitchy" in a TV interview. He agreed and said that this was something he had in common with the BFG, who couldn't stand "doing nothing."

The Twits ~ This is a book best read while holding your nose. Mr. and Mrs. Twit are truly disgusting and magnificently foul—a real toe-curler!

U is for ...

uckyslush
umpossible
ucky-mucky

Upside down ~ In Roald Dahl's books, many things are topsy-turvy. Mr. and Mrs. Twit cruelly force their monkeys to live upside down. The Minpins wear suction boots that allow them to walk up trees. And Roald once wrote a short story called **The Upside Down Mice**. This appeared in the **Puffin Annual** in 1974, and it's about an old man named Labon who is pestered by mice in his house. Does this snippet remind you of any other Roald story you might have read?

When Labon came down the next morning and saw that there were no mice caught in the traps, he smiled but said nothing.

He took a chair and put glue on the bottom of its legs and stuck it upside down to the ceiling, near the mousetraps.

He did the same with the table, the television set and the lamp. He took everything that was on the floor and stuck it upside down on the ceiling. He even put a little carpet up there.

The next night, when the mice came out of their holes, they were still joking and laughing about what they had seen the night before. But now, when they looked up at the ceiling, they stopped laughing very suddenly.

"Good gracious me!" cried one. "Look up there! There's the floor!"

"Heavens above!" shouted another. "We must be standing on the ceiling."

Random Roald Fact

He would have loved to
have seen a ghost and to
have written a ghost story.
He tried, but never managed it.

V is for ...

Vegetables ~ These were Roald Dahl's favorite things to grow and eat—apart from chocolate, of course. He thought that broad beans and onions were scrumdiddlyumptious.

A very important meeting ~ In 1942, C. S. Forester—an author of swashbuckling adventure stories—took Roald Dahl to lunch to interview him about his wartime experiences for the **Saturday Evening Post**. Roald was thrilled to be meeting such a famous author, and lunch got in the way, so Forester didn't end up with any notes. When he got home, Roald put pen to paper and wrote a story that he sent to Forester. And what did the swashbuckling author do? He sent Roald's work to a magazine, and it was published just as Roald had written it! Roald was paid $1,000 and he gave ten percent of this to Forester's agent. If the two men had not met, Roald might never have become a writer. . . . Imagine that! (Actually, don't.)

The very young ~ Roald Dahl thought that writing for very young children was one of the most difficult things to do. Of his own picture books, he was most pleased with **The Enormous Crocodile** and **The Giraffe and the Pelly and Me**.

The Vicar of Nibbleswicke ~ The rights for this book were auctioned off to raise money for the Dyslexia Institute. A video recording of Roald—speaking from his hospital bed—was played at the auction. The proceeds from **The Vicar of Nibbleswicke** continue to support children with reading difficulties.

Vices ~ According to Liccy Dahl his worst vice was smoking and his second was . . . smoking in bed!

Virtues ~ Roald Dahl's best qualities were his generosity and the ability to *never* be boring.

Vocabulary ~ Roald Dahl was passionate about words and he would tell you that the best way to learn lovely words was to read as much as possible. He thought that nothing encouraged a love of words more than stories and reading, and he did his utmost to make sure that his own books were unputdownable. Written in 1930, when he was 14, this description of a teacher reveals Roald's early talent for word magic:

> **"He's a short man with a face like a fried elderberry, and a moustache which closely resembles the African jungle."**
> — ROALD DAHL

Random
Roald Fact

He used to announce that
meals were ready by shouting,
"Nosebags on!" or, "Grub's up!"

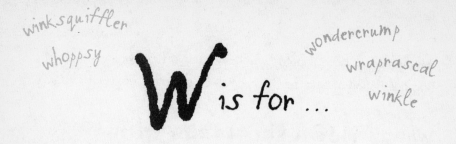

winksquiffler
whoppsy

W is for ...

wondercrump
wraprascal
winkle

Washington ~ Roald Dahl spent happy times working in the U.S. capital in the 1940s. He loved the social life, meeting many famous people—diplomats, movie stars, writers, and even presidents.

Waterproof ~ When he was a very small boy, Roald Dahl would lie in the bath worrying that his skin would develop a leak and he would fill up with water and sink, or even die. When he discovered the truth, he marveled at his waterproof skin.

Did You Know?
Between 30,000 and 40,000
skin cells fall from your
body every minute.

Where the Wild Things Are ~ Maurice Sendak was lined up to illustrate the American edition of **Charlie and the Chocolate Factory**, but the success of his now classic picture book **Where the Wild**

Things Are meant that he was too busy and too expensive for the job. What would his illustrations have looked like? We'll never know. . . .

Whitbread Best Children's Novel ~ In 1983, this

was won by (drum roll, please . . .) **The Witches**! Roald Dahl was utterly delighted to win, especially because he thought that the Whitbread Awards were the very best of the literary awards. He gave his prize money to the Oxford Hospice for sick children.

Whizzpops ~ One of Roald Dahl's dinner guests had

peculiar table manners. After dessert, he would entertain everyone else by lighting his own whizzpops. (And if you don't know what whizzpops are, you'll have to read **The BFG**.)

WARNING!
Don't try this at home.

Did You Know?

Whizzpopping is caused by the 200 or so bacteria in your large intestine that work on the carbohydrates not properly digested in your stomach. In breaking down these carbohydrates, they give off gases such as methane and hydrogen. Hydrogen sulphide is the gas responsible for the stinky smell.

Wine ~ Roald Dahl was fascinated by wine as a young man and started collecting it in the late 1940s, when it wasn't very expensive to buy. The cellar under Gipsy House held around 4,000 bottles and was just the right temperature (55°F, year-round). Roald had a special wooden chute built for big deliveries.

Wine gums ~ Roald Dahl loved these candies and, as an adult, kept a large jar of them by his bed in case he was hungry in the night.

Winkles ~ To enjoy these tiny creatures the Roald Dahl way, just follow these instructions:

1. Collect periwinkles from rocky seaside places (while on a holiday in Tenby, South Wales, if you want to be just like Roald Dahl).
2. Boil them.
3. Pry each one from its shell using a bent pin.
4. Pile on top of bread and butter.
5. Gobble them up.

Witch balls ~ Roald Dahl's children had fifty different-colored glass balls hanging from their bedroom ceilings. These were witch balls. Roald said that if a witch came into the room she would see her reflection in the balls and flee at the sight of her own ugliness, never to return. When Ophelia heard the wind howling in the trees at night, she always thought it was a witch wailing in anger after seeing her ghastly reflection in the balls. . . .

> **" The stories he told us always had a spooky edge. "**
> —OPHELIA DAHL

The Witches

The Witches ~ The ideas for **The Witches** came from all of the Norwegian fairy tales told to Roald Dahl by his Norwegian grandparents. This brilliant book, which won the Whitbread Award in 1983, has the most unusual ending.

Witch's Tree ~ Near Roald Dahl's home, Gipsy House, there was a huge old beech tree known to locals as the Witch's Tree. But Roald knew that the tree would suit a fox far better than a nasty old witch. So this is the home of the particularly clever and cunning Fantastic Mr. Fox. Sadly, disaster struck in 2004 and the 150-year-old tree fell and died in a storm.

The Wonderful Story of Henry Sugar and Six more ~ In the title story of this collection, millionaire gambler Henry Sugar gives all his winnings to orphanages. And in real life, Roald Dahl was equally concerned about orphaned children—he was a patron of the Dr Barnardo's charity, a foundation that works to improve children's lives, for many years.

World Book Day ~ In 1999, **Matilda** was voted the most
popular children's book in a World Book Day survey involving 15,000
seven- to eleven-year-olds. Hooray!

World-famous explorer ~ Roald Dahl was named after
the first person to reach the South Pole. Norwegian explorer Roald
Amundsen was one of his father's heroes.

WOW! ~ Roald Dahl's father lost his arm in a horrific accident when he
was fourteen, but despite this he was an amazing woodcarver. He said the
only real inconvenience was that he couldn't cut the top off his boiled egg.
He could, however, tie his shoes single-handed. See if you can do it!

Writing board ~ Roald Dahl designed and made a writing board that suited him perfectly. It was a shaped board covered with green baize (a type of felt material), which he fixed at exactly the right angle for him to rest his paper on and write in comfort. It was the only thing in the Hut that was cleaned regularly. Roald used an old clothes brush to sweep off the scraps of rubber that gathered after endless rubbings-out of his pencilled words. The rubbings would fall on the floor, which was never swept.

Wrong number ~ When Roald Dahl's first American publisher, Alfred Knopf, first called him to say he'd like to publish one of his books, Roald was so surprised, he almost hung up, thinking it was a joke caller. Phew!

www.roalddahl.com ~ Roald Dahl has his own totally terrific Web site. You'd be a snozzcumber to miss it.

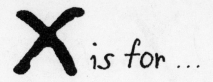

X is for ...

X-rays ~ Roald Dahl's insides were photographed many times, as doctors tried to find out exactly what was wrong with his back and work out how to make it better.

Did You Know?

X-rays were discovered by German physicist Wilhelm Roentgen, almost by accident, in 1895. When the rays pass through objects (e.g., the human body), some substances are more resistant to them than others (e.g., bones). If you put a piece of film behind the object you are X-raying, the bits that the rays don't pass through form a shadow on the film.

Y is for ...

Yawning ~ (Isn't it funny how just reading that word makes you want to open your mouth wide and y-a-a-a-w-n?) Roald Dahl hated being bored. (Maybe this is why his books are never boring!) He was very bad at stifling his yawns when he found things dreary and dull. A TV presenter once noticed him yawning during a live interview and asked if he was bored. Never one to mince his words, Roald answered, "Yes."

Yellow paper ~ Roald Dahl wrote all of his books on American yellow legal pads, which were sent to him from New York. Perhaps this is why yellow was his favorite color.

Yellow pencils ~ Roald Dahl always wrote in pencil and only ever used a very particular kind of yellow pencil with an eraser on the end—a Dixon Ticonderoga 1388-2 5/10, medium. Before he started a writing session, Roald made sure he had six sharpened pencils in a jar by his side. They lasted for two hours before needing to be resharpened.

Z is for ...

zoop
zozimus
zippfizzing

Zippfizzing ~ This is the BFG's word for the nightly journeys the bad giants take to countries all around the world to "guzzle human beans."

Zoo ~ Next time you go to the zoo, keep your parents away from escaped rhinoceroses, or you could end up like James.

Roald Dahl's Children's Books

Novels

THE BFG (1982)

BOY: TALES OF CHILDHOOD (1984)

CHARLIE AND THE CHOCOLATE FACTORY (1964)

CHARLIE AND THE GREAT GLASS ELEVATOR (1972)

DANNY THE CHAMPION OF THE WORLD (1975)

GEORGE'S MARVELLOUS MEDICINE (1981)

GOING SOLO (1986)

JAMES AND THE GIANT PEACH (1961)

MATILDA (1988)

THE WITCHES (1983)

Cookbooks

THE GREMLINS (1993)

REVOLTING RECIPES (1994)

EVEN MORE REVOLTING RECIPES (2001)

RHYME STEW (1989)

Teenage Fiction

THE GREAT AUTOMATIC GRAMMATIZATOR AND OTHER STORIES, published in the U.S. as THE UMBRELLA MAN (1996)

SKIN AND OTHER STORIES (2000)

THE VICAR OF NIBBLESWICKE (1991)

THE WONDERFUL STORY OF HENRY SUGAR AND SIX MORE (1977)

For younger Readers

THE ENORMOUS CROCODILE (1978)

ESIO TROT (1990)

FANTASTIC MR. FOX (1970)

THE GIRAFFE AND THE PELLY AND ME (1985)

THE MAGIC FINGER (1966)

THE TWITS (1980)

Picture books

THE MINPINS with Patrick Benson (1991)

Poems

DIRTY BEASTS with Quentin Blake (1983)

REVOLTING RHYMES with Quentin Blake (1982)

Plays

THE BFG: PLAYS FOR CHILDREN Adapted by David Wood (1993)

CHARLIE AND THE CHOCOLATE FACTORY: A PLAY Adapted by Richard George (1976)

CHARLIE AND THE GREAT GLASS ELEVATOR : A PLAY Adapted by Richard George (1984)

FANTASTIC MR. FOX: A PLAY Adapted by Sally Reid (1987)

JAMES AND THE GIANT PEACH: A PLAY Adapted by Richard George (1982)

THE TWITS: PLAYS FOR CHILDREN Adapted by David Wood (2003)

THE WITCHES: PLAYS FOR CHILDREN Adapted by David Wood (2001)

There's more to Roald Dahl than great stories...

Did you know that 10% of author royalties* from this book go to help the work of the Roald Dahl charities?

The Roald Dahl Foundation supports specialist pediatric Roald Dahl nurses throughout the UK caring for children with epilepsy, blood disorders, and acquired brain injury. It also provides practical help for children and young people with brain, blood, and literacy problems—all causes close to Roald Dahl during his lifetime—through grants to UK hospitals and charities as well as to individual children and their families.

The Roald Dahl Museum and Story Centre, based in Great Missenden just outside London, is in the Buckinghamshire village where Roald Dahl lived and wrote. At the heart of the Museum, created to inspire a love of reading and writing, is his unique archive of letters and manuscripts. As well as two fun-packed biographical galleries, the Museum boasts an interactive Story Centre. It is a place for family, teachers and their pupils to explore the exciting world of creativity and literacy.

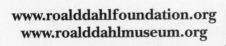

www.roalddahlfoundation.org
www.roalddahlmuseum.org